International Labour

69th Session   1983

Report III

(Part 4 B)

Third Item on the Agenda:
Information and Reports on the Application
of Conventions and Recommendations

General Survey on the Application of the Conventions on Freedom of Association, the Right to Organise and Collective Bargaining and the Convention and Recommendation concerning Rural Workers' Organisations

Report of the Committee of Experts on the Application of Conventions and
Recommendations (Articles 19, 22 and 35 of the Constitution)/volume B

International Labour Office

525473

ISBN 92-2-103128-4
ISSN 0074-6681

First published 1983

Printed in Switzerland

TABLE OF CONTENTS

        Sanctions 222-223

CHAPTER VIII: DISSOLUTION AND SUSPENSION OF ORGANISATIONS . 227-235

CHAPTER IX: RIGHT OF ORGANISATIONS TO ESTABLISH AND JOIN
               FEDERATIONS AND CONFEDERATIONS AND TO
               AFFILIATE WITH INTERNATIONAL ORGANISATIONS 236-252

        Right of federation and confederation 238-249

           Minimum number of member organisations   240

           Limited affiliation 241-245

           Limitation of the right to federate and
           confederate of specific categories of
           trade unions 246-249

        International affiliation 250-251

               THE RIGHT TO ORGANISE AND COLLECTIVE
                          BARGAINING 253-319

        Introduction 253-255

CHAPTER X: PROTECTION AGAINST ACTS OF ANTI-UNION
               DISCRIMINATION 256-280

        The period covered and persons protected 259-263

        Enforcement procedures 264-278

CHAPTER XI: PROTECTION AGAINST ACTS OF INTERFERENCE 281-285

CHAPTER XII: PROMOTION OF COLLECTIVE BARGAINING 286-319

        Promotion 292-302

           Recognition of trade unions for the purpose of
           collective bargaining 293-297

           Machinery and procedures to facilitate bargaining .. 298-302

        Voluntary bargaining - autonomy of the parties 303-315

                 ORGANISATIONS OF RURAL WORKERS   320-365

CHAPTER XIII: RURAL WORKERS' ORGANISATIONS 320-365

        ILO standards other than the Convention and
        Recommendation concerning rural workers'
        organisations 323-326

CHAPTER I

General introduction

Background to the Survey

1.   In accordance with article 19 of the Constitution of the
International Labour Organisation, the Governing Body of the
International Labour Office decided at its 214th Session (November
1980) to request reports on the following instruments from States which
have not ratified them:

- the Freedom of Association and Protection of the Right to
  Organise Convention, 1948 (No. 87);

- the Right to Organise and Collective Bargaining Convention, 1949
  (No. 98);

- the Rural Workers' Organisations Convention, 1975 (No. 141),

and to ask all member States to supply reports on the Rural Workers'
Organisations Recommendation, 1975 (No. 149).

2.   These reports on the position of law and practice in regard
to the standards contained in the aforementioned instruments, together
with those submitted in accordance with article 22 of the Constitution
by States which have ratified one or more of these Conventions, have
provided an opportunity for the Committee of Experts on the Application
of Conventions and Recommendations, in accordance with its usual
practice, to make a general survey of the situation.

3.   The present survey is the fifth of its kind on Conventions
No. 87 and No. 98 and the first on Convention No. 141 and Recommendation No. 149. The previous general surveys on freedom of association
and collective bargaining were made in 1959 and 1973; reports on these
two instruments had already been examined separately in 1956 and 1957.

International sources of law
respecting trade union rights

Principal source: the ILO

Basic standards

4.   As an essential condition for the defence of workers and
forming, as it does, a part of basic human rights, freedom of
association assumes special importance for the ILO in view of the
Organisation's unique tripartite structure. Owing its existence

largely to the will and efforts of the trade union organisations, the ILO could not fail to recognise in its Constitution of 1919 the principle of freedom of association as one of the objectives of its programme of action. The Preamble to Part XIII of the Treaty of Versailles mentioned "recognition of the principle of freedom of association" among the objects to be promoted by the Organisation, and the general principles set forth in Article 427 contained a provision concerning "the right of association for all lawful purposes by the employed as well as by the employers".

5.   At the end of the Second World War the Constitution of the ILO was supplemented by the inclusion of the Declaration of Philadelphia which reaffirmed the fundamental nature of this principle by stressing that "freedom of expression and of association are essential for sustained progress". At the same time, this Declaration cited, among the programmes whose implementation had to be furthered, those which will achieve "the effective recognition of the right of collective bargaining, the co-operation of management and labour in the continuous improvement of productive efficiency, and the collaboration of workers and employers in the preparation and application of social and economic measures". The principles enunciated in the Constitution are applicable to all the member States of the Organisation.

6.   Freedom of association having thus been proclaimed from the outset as one of the fundamental principles of the Organisation, the need was rapidly felt, particularly among the workers' representatives, to define this general concept more precisely and to set forth its essential elements in an ILO instrument in order that its application could be effectively promoted and supervised.

7.   In 1927 the International Labour Conference discussed a draft international instrument on freedom of association, but without result.[1] The project only materialised after the Second World War: in 1948 the International Labour Conference adopted the Freedom of Association and Protection of the Right to Organise Convention (No. 87) and the following year, the Right to Organise and Collective Bargaining Convention (No. 98), which are the basic instruments relating to freedom of association.[2]

8.   Of the other instruments adopted by the ILO bearing upon trade union rights, the following can be singled out for particular attention:

    - in chronological order, the earliest ILO Convention to deal with the right to organise was the Right of Association (Agriculture) Convention, 1921 (No. 11): without defining this right, it provides that all persons engaged in agriculture shall possess the same rights of association and combination as industrial workers. The discussions at the International Labour Conference at the time of the adoption of this Convention make it possible to establish clearly that the provisions of the Convention are applicable not only to agricultural wage earners but also to sharecroppers, tenants, small independent peasants and other categories of agricultural workers;

----

[1] The placing of this item on the agenda of the 1928 Session of the International Labour Conference was rejected by the Workers' group, mainly because of questions relating to the right not to organise and the legal formalities to be observed by organisations.

[2] For a detailed description of the content of these Conventions, see below, paras. 45 to 47 and paras. 253 to 255.

- in 1947 the Conference adopted the Right of Association (Non-Metropolitan Territories) Convention (No. 84), which deals in general terms with the right to organise, collective bargaining, consultation with organisations of employers and workers and procedures for the investigation of industrial disputes in these territories.

9.   Collective bargaining and the settlement of disputes were the subject of two separate instruments in 1951:

- the Collective Agreements Recommendation (No. 91) dealing with collective bargaining machinery, definition of collective agreements, effects of such agreements, their extension, their interpretation and supervision of their application;

- the Voluntary Conciliation and Arbitration Recommendation (No. 92) which is aimed at promoting the establishment of voluntary conciliation machinery in which employers and workers are equally represented; it stresses the voluntary nature of conciliation and arbitration procedures by specifying that none of its provisions may be interpreted as limiting the right to strike.

10.   Other instruments are aimed at institutionalising consultation at various levels in the field of industrial relations:

- the Co-operation at the Level of the Undertaking Recommendation, 1952 (No. 94) is aimed at encouraging consultation at the workplace;

- the Consultation (Industrial and National Levels) Recommendation, 1960 (No. 113), for its part, covers consultation at higher levels, the parties concerned being the public authorities and employers' and workers' organisations. The general objective of such consultation should be to promote mutual understanding and good relations between the authorities and employers' and workers' organisations, as well as between these organisations themselves.

11.   The functions of employers' and workers' organisations and their representatives in examining workers' grievances at the undertaking level are dealt with in the Examination of Grievances Recommendation, 1967 (No. 130).

12.   Still in the field of employer-worker relations at the level of the undertaking, the Workers' Representatives Convention, 1971 (No. 135) and the accompanying Recommendation (No. 143) contain specific provisions for the protection of such representatives (trade union representatives or representatives elected by the workers of the undertaking) against any act prejudicial to them, including dismissal, based on their status or activities as workers' representatives or on union membership or participation in union activities; these instruments also provide that such representatives shall also be afforded facilities in the undertaking in order to enable them to carry out their functions promptly and efficiently.

13.   It was in 1975 that the International Labour Conference adopted the Rural Workers' Organisations Convention (No. 141) and Recommendation (No. 149) to take into account the difficulties

encountered by these workers in the exercise of their trade union rights.[1]

14. The Convention (No. 151) and Recommendation (No. 159) concerning protection of the right to organise and procedures for determining conditions of employment in the public service were adopted in 1978.[2]

15. Finally, in 1981 the International Labour Conference adopted the Collective Bargaining Convention (No. 154) and Recommendation (No. 163).[3]

16. In addition to Conventions and Recommendations the International Labour Conference has adopted a number of resolutions relating to freedom of association. The Committee of Experts is particularly anxious to highlight the 1952 resolution concerning independence of the trade union movement and the 1970 resolution concerning trade union rights and their relation to civil liberties; the latter recognises that the rights conferred upon workers' and employers' organisations must be based on respect for those civil liberties which have been enunciated in particular in the Universal Declaration of Human Rights and in the International Covenant on Civil and Political Rights, adding that the absence of these civil liberties removes all meaning from the concept of trade union rights. It places special emphasis on civil liberties which it declares are essential for the normal exercise of trade union rights.[4]

Principles and practice

17. The ILO standards on trade union matters have been supplemented and developed by the principles enunciated by a number of bodies, in particular the Governing Body Committee on Freedom of Association and the Fact-Finding and Conciliation Commission on Freedom of Association set up to promote and supervise the application of these standards. These principles are properly regarded as constituting a body of accepted case law in the field of freedom of association and are so applied.[5]

Other international sources of law in the field of trade union rights

18. Although the United Nations does not deal with labour questions as such, and in an agreement concluded in 1946 with the ILO, it had recognised the latter as the specialised agency with responsibility for taking appropriate measures to achieve the objectives laid down in its Constitution, it has adopted, within the framework of instruments of a more general scope, standards also concerning labour matters, including trade union rights. The instruments in question are mainly those relating to human rights.

----

[1] For a detailed description of the content of these instruments, see below, paras. 327 to 332.

[2] See below, para. 20.

[3] See below, para. 20.

[4] See below, para. 52.

[5] See below, paras. 28 to 30.

19. The 1948 Universal Declaration of Human Rights, the 1966 International Covenant on Economic, Social and Cultural Rights and the 1966 International Covenant and Protocol on Civil and Political Rights established the fundamental civil liberties which form part of human rights and which are essential for the free exercise of trade union rights. The Universal Declaration of Human Rights provides, inter alia, that everyone has the right to form and to join trade unions for the protection of his interests; the Covenants, which entered into force in 1976, contain provisions concerning the right of association and in particular the right to form trade unions and to strike. In accordance with article 18 of the International Covenant on Economic, Social and Cultural Rights, the International Labour Organisation reports to the Economic and Social Council of the United Nations on the progress made in achieving the observance of the provisions of the Covenant falling within the scope of the Organisation's activities. The Governing Body entrusted this task to the Committee of Experts which has examined, at its sessions from 1978 to 1982, the position in a number of States Parties to the Covenant with respect to the implementation of, in particular, article 8 of the Covenant.[1]

ILO action since 1973[2]

20. Freedom of association and protection of the right to organise form part of the basic human rights which the ILO has assumed a solemn obligation to further among the nations of the world. The Committee of Experts notes that, since 1973, the ILC has continued to increase its efforts in this field through both its standard-setting activities and the decisions of its supervisory bodies.

Standards:

- the Rural Workers' Organisations Convention (No. 141) and Recommendation (No. 149) - which, together with Conventions Nos. 87 and 98, form the subject of this survey - were adopted in 1975. These instruments, recognising the fundamental principles of freedom of association and the right of rural workers to organise, provide that member States shall adopt and carry out a policy of active encouragement to rural workers' organisations, particularly with a view to eliminating obstacles to their establishment, their growth and the pursuit of their lawful activities, as well as such legislative and administrative discrimination against these organisations and their members as may exist[3] (23 countries have ratified Convention No. 141);

- the Labour Relations (Public Service) Convention (No. 151) and Recommendation (No. 159) were adopted in 1978 to take into account the problems encountered by public employees in exercising their trade union rights (15 countries have ratified Convention No. 151);

---

[1] See ILO: Report of the Committee of Experts on the Application of Conventions and Recommendations (RCE), Report III (Part 4A), International Labour Conference (ILC), 68th Session, Geneva, 1982, para. 15.

[2] The date of the last general survey.

[3] See below, Chapter XIII.

- the Collective Bargaining Convention (No. 154) and Recommendation (No. 163), adopted in 1981, are aimed at furthering the achievement of the objectives of a number of standards adopted by the International Labour Conference, and particularly the general principles set forth in Article 4 of Convention No. 98, by appropriate measures based on these standards and aimed at promoting free and voluntary collective bargaining (three countries have ratified Convention No. 154).[1]

Promotion and supervision machinery

21.   In view of the importance of the standards and principles relating to freedom of association, the Committee of Experts recalls that the ILO has established, independently of the general procedures applicable to all international labour Conventions, special procedures solely for questions relating to trade union rights.

General procedures

22.   The general procedures are of two types, the first being of a regular and automatic nature and the second based on the submission of complaints.

23.   The regular procedure mainly consists in supervision of the application of ratified Conventions by the Committee of Experts on the Application of Conventions and Recommendations and the Committee on the Application of Conventions and Recommendations of the International Labour Conference. The Committee of Experts observes that the freedom of association Conventions, in view of both their content and the number of observations to which they give rise, continue to constitute one of the most important aspects of the work of these two bodies.

24.   The procedure based on complaints is set in motion when a representation (article 24 of the Constitution) or a complaint (article 26 of the Constitution) is made alleging that a State is not applying a Convention it has ratified in a satisfactory manner. Representations are examined by a tripartite working party, comprising three persons - one government member, one worker and one employer - set up by the Governing Body and chosen from within its membership.[2] In cases where the Governing Body finds the Government's reply unsatisfactory it may decide to publish the text of the representation, the Government's reply and the conclusions of the working party. When a complaint is submitted, the Governing Body may appoint a Commission of Inquiry, composed of independent persons, to consider the complaint and to report thereon. The Government concerned must indicate whether or not it accepts the recommendations of the Commission of Inquiry; if it does not, it may refer the dispute to the International Court of Justice.

25.   In the field of freedom of association, this procedure had been used in the case of Greece, after several delegates to the
----

[1] This Convention will come into force on 11 August 1983.

[2] If the representation concerns one of the freedom of association Conventions it may be referred to the Committee on Freedom of Association for examination in accordance with articles 24 and 25 of the Constitution (see para. 29 below).

International Labour Conference had submitted complaints against that country in 1968. The Greek Government accepted the recommendations contained in the report of the Commission of Inquiry.[1]

26.   Recently, the Governing Body set up a Commission of Inquiry following the submission of complaints concerning the application of certain Conventions, including Conventions Nos. 87 and 98, by Workers' delegates to the 67th Session (1981) of the Conference against the Governments of Haiti and the Dominican Republic.

27.   In other cases, the Governing Body decided to co-ordinate the procedure with that being followed for complaints already pending before the Committee on Freedom of Association. This was the case following the submission of a complaint (under article 26) to the 60th Session (1975) of the Conference concerning the application by Bolivia of Convention No. 87. The examination of this complaint was completed in 1978. An identical procedure was followed by the Governing Body in respect of complaints (under article 26) submitted in 1976 and 1977 against Uruguay and Argentina respectively and in 1982 against Poland, as well as the representation (under article 24) presented in 1982 against Turkey.

Special procedures

28.   Special procedures for the protection of freedom of association were envisaged at the time the International Labour Conference was discussing Conventions Nos. 87 and 98, since, under the general procedures described above, if a State did not ratify these Conventions it was impossible to supervise their application, despite the great importance attached to respect for the standards and principles relating to trade union rights. Consequently, in agreement with the Economic and Social Council of the United Nations (ECOSOC), the Fact-Finding and Conciliation Commission on Freedom of Association was set up in 1950.[2] Under the terms of its mandate, this body examines complaints of violations of trade union rights referred to it by the Governing Body concerning countries belonging to the ILO which have or have not ratified the freedom of association Conventions. This procedure requires the prior consent of the government concerned.[3] Complaints submitted against States Members of the United Nations but which are not Members of the International Labour Organisation are transmitted to the Commission if the government concerned so agrees. Composed of independent persons nominated by the Governing Body, this Commission is essentially an investigatory body, but it can examine, together with the government concerned, the possibilities of settling the difficulties involved by agreement. As a general rule, it functions as panels of three members. The Commission, which was first

---

[1] ILO: Official Bulletin (O.B.), Special Supplement, Vol. LIV, No. 2, 1971.

[2] Economic and Social Council Resolutions Nos. 239(IX) of 2 August 1949 and 277(X) dated 17 February 1950; 110th Session of the Governing Body, Official Minutes, pp. 71-9C.

[3] The only exception is in respect of any complaint relating to the application of a ratified Convention in the case of which the Governing Body may designate the Fact-Finding and Conciliation Commission as a Commission of Inquiry under article 26 of the Constitution of the International Labour Organisation.

convened in 1964, had dealt with two cases up to 1973 (Japan, Greece).[1]
It has functioned three times since 1973[2] in cases concerning,
respectively, Chile (State Member of the ILO not having ratified
Conventions Nos. 87 and 98), Lesotho and the United States (Puerto
Rico) (States which were not Members of the ILO at the time the
complaints were submitted).[3] The Fact-Finding and Conciliation
Commission has been convened only rarely, mainly because of the fact
that, prior to 1964, no government that had been requested to do so had
given its consent.

29.   On the other hand, the cases submitted to and examined by
the Committee on Freedom of Association of the Governing Body of the
ILO have been constantly increasing in number in recent years. The
Committee was established in November 1951 as a tripartite body
composed of nine members of the Governing Body. The Committee deals
with complaints filed against countries which have, or have not,
ratified the freedom of association Conventions. The legal basis for
this concept is the Constitution of the ILO and the Declaration of
Philadelphia according to which States, by their membership of the
Organisation, are bound to respect the principles contained in the
Constitution, including that concerning freedom of association. The
consent of the governments concerned is not necessary for these
complaints to be examined. The Committee systematically examines the
substance of the cases submitted to it and presents conclusions
thereon, recommending the Governing Body to draw the attention of the
governments concerned to any principles called into question in the
matter and in particular any recommendations made with a view to the
settlement of the questions raised in the complaint. To be receivable
complaints submitted to the ILO must emanate from a national
organisation directly concerned, an international organisation of
workers or employers having consultative status with the ILO, or other
international organisations of employers and workers where the
allegations relate to matters directly affecting an organisation
affiliated to them. The complaints must be submitted in writing, duly
signed by a representative of an organisation authorised to submit them
and supported as completely as possible with proof of the allegations
concerning specific infringements of trade union rights. The Committee
on Freedom of Association has adopted supplementary rules of procedure
on various occasions, the last time being in 1979 with a view to
strengthening the procedure for examining complaints and which covered
the following matters: relations with complainants and governments,
urgent and non-urgent reports, missions on the spot and hearing of the
parties.[4]

30.   Since 1973 more than 400 new cases - 70 during the last

----

[1] Japan: ILO: O.B., Special Supplement, Vol. LIX, No. 1, 1966;
Greece: ILO: O.B., Special Supplement, Vol. LIX, No. 3, 1966.

[2] Chile: ILO: The trade union situation in Chile (Geneva, 1975);
Lesotho: Governing Body document (GB.197/3/5); United States (Puerto
Rico): Governing Body document (GB.218/7/2).

[3] The United States and Lesotho rejoined the ILO in 1980.

[4] 193rd Report of the Committee on Freedom of Association approved
by the Governing Body at its 210th Session (May 1979), ILO: C.B., Vol.
LXII, 1979, Series B, No. 1.

year alone - have been submitted to the Committee on Freedom of Association.[1]

Direct contacts and other on-the-spot visits

31.   In 1967 the Committee of Experts, anxious to make its working methods more efficient, and aware that the absence of direct contacts with the governments concerned or of direct knowledge of the situations under consideration might give rise to prolonged difficulties, considered whether certain additional procedures might not make possible a fuller examination of issues and a more fruitful dialogue with governments. Thus originated the idea - which was subsequently developed - of direct contacts with governments - the relevant procedure being elaborated by the Committee of Experts in 1968, 1972 and 1973 - with the aim of promoting and widening on a verbal basis the dialogue that was originally based on written comments. Direct contacts, which take place outside any strict formalism, basically involve a visit to the country concerned - with the consent of the government concerned - by a representative of the ILO (an independent person or an official of the Office) to discuss the problem involved with government representatives and workers' and employers' organisations, to make known the opinion of the supervisory bodies, to gain full information on the position of both sides and on the nature of the difficulties encountered (both in the application of ratified Conventions and other standard-related questions) and to present the Committee of Experts with the information thus gathered.

32.   In 1979 the Committee of Experts reviewed[2] the experience gained and the results achieved through direct contacts and noted that this procedure had achieved very positive results. The Conference Committee also recognised that positive results had been obtained by this procedure.

33.   In the specific field of freedom of association, a number of direct contacts have taken place in connection with the observance of constitutional obligations and the application of Conventions, with particular reference to the Conventions on freedom of association or a group of Conventions of which those on freedom of association formed part.

34.   In addition, the direct contacts procedure has been developed particularly within the framework of the proceedings of the Committee on Freedom of Association. Since these proceedings are based almost exclusively on written communications, it was deemed necessary to supplement them in certain appropriate cases with a procedure allowing for on-the-spot visits, discussions and examination of situations.[3]

----

[1] The significant decisions taken by the Committee have been published in ILO: Freedom of association; Digest of decisions of the Freedom of Association Committee (Geneva, 1976, 2nd revised edition).

[2] ILO: RCE, Report III (Part 4A), 1979, paras. 42-89.

[3] Such visits had been made as long ago as 1962 to Libya and Costa Rica. In each case, on the invitation of the governments concerned, an independent person, accompanied by an ILO official, travelled to the country and, after various interviews with all concerned, submitted a detailed report to the Committee indicating the facts it had been able to establish and how the situation was progressing.

35.   The general idea behind these various contacts is the same as for the application of Conventions in general, but the procedure followed in freedom of association matters nevertheless has a number of distinctive features since cases concerning freedom of association are generally of an urgent nature and frequently concern questions of fact rather than conformity of legislation.

36.   The Committee on Freedom of Association has drawn up rules governing "direct contacts" missions. The procedure consists in sending a representative of the Director-General of the ILO to the country to obtain the pertinent facts in the matter and to seek possible solutions to the difficulties encountered either during the examination of the case or at the follow-up stage of the Governing Body's recommendations with the proviso that such contacts are established only at the invitation of the government concerned or with its consent. Where complaints are of an urgent nature the Director-General of the ILO may, with the approval of the chairman of the Committee, suggest to the government concerned that this procedure should be set in motion without waiting for a meeting of the Committee. Direct contacts are not limited to on-the-spot visits by a representative of the Director-General. The system is broadly applied to permit appearances to be made before the Committee on Freedom of Association of representatives of the governments concerned.

37.   Since 1973 on-the-spot visits have been undertaken in 1974 (Jordan) and in 1975 (Uruguay); in 1976, there were two (both in Bolivia); in 1977 another one (again in Uruguay) and, in 1978, five (Argentina, Chile, Dominican Republic, United Kingdom/Antigua and Tunisia); in 1979, one (Sri Lanka); in 1980, eight (Argentina, Bolivia, Chile, E+hiopia, Poland (twice), Tunisia and USSR); in 1981, five (Nicaragua, Poland, Tunisia and two in Uruguay); in 1982, two (Poland and Turkey).

Studies on freedom of association

38.   Since 1973 in response mainly to the views expressed by the International Labour Conference in its Resolution concerning trade union rights and their relation to civil liberties,[1] the ILO has published a number of separate studies on certain aspects of freedom of association.[2]

State of ratifications

39.   As of March 1983 Convention No. 87 has been ratified by 96 countries, Convention No. 98 by 112 countries and Convention No. 141 by

---

[1] ILO: Record of Proceedings, ILC, 54th Session, Geneva, 1970, p. 733.

[2] Eligibility for Trade Union Office (Geneva, ILO, 1972); The public authorities and the right to protection of trade union funds and property (Geneva, ILO, 1973); H.G. Bartoloméi de la Cruz: Protection against anti-union discrimination (Geneva, ILO, 1976); Guy Caire: Freedom of Association and economic development (Geneva, ILO, 1976); Bernard Gernigon: Tenure of trade union office (Geneva, ILO, 1977); Jay A. Erstling; The right to organise (Geneva, ILO, 1977); Jean-Michel Servais: Inviolability of trade union premises and communications (Geneva, ILO, 1979). See also the workers' education manual entitled: Trade unions and the ILO, published in 1979.

23 countries. Since 1973 17 countries have ratified Convention No. 87
and 20 have ratified Convention No. 98.

Information available

40.   The present survey is based both on reports supplied under
article 19 of the ILO Constitution by countries which have not ratified
the Conventions concerned and on the reports supplied under article 22
of the Constitution by countries bound by these instruments. The total
number of reports supplied under article 19 is 27 in respect of the
Freedom of Association and Protection of the Right to Organise
Convention, 1948 (No. 87), 20 in respect of the Right to Organise and
Collective Bargaining Convention, 1949 (No. 98), 77 for the Rural
Workers' Organisations Convention, 1975 (No. 141) and 86 for the Rural
Workers' Organisations Recommendation, 1975 (No. 149).   Detailed
information regarding the countries which have supplied these reports,
as well as of the countries for which information has been available in
reports supplied under article 22, will be found in Appendix II to this
survey. The total number of countries whose reports have been taken
into consideration in the preparation of this survey is 139.   The
Committee, in addition to examining the information contained in the
reports, has also sought to take account of relevant legislation and
practice.   In 14 cases it noted comments which had been made by
workers' organisations. The Committee must note, however, that it has
sometimes been difficult to gather information on the practical
application of Conventions and even, in some cases, to obtain all of
the national legislation pertaining to the matters dealt with in the
present study. This is especially the case as regards non-metropolitan
territories, for which the Committee has very little information at its
disposal on the practices followed.

Arrangement of the survey

41.   The present general survey is divided into three parts
dealing, respectively, with the Freedom of Association and Protection
of the Right to Organise Convention, 1948 (No. 87); the Right to
Organise and Collective Bargaining Convention, 1949 (No. 98); and the
Rural Workers' Organisations Convention (No. 141) and Recommendation
(No. 149) of 1975.

*
* *

42.   A member of the Committee, Mr. Ivanov, stated that he did
not share the interpretation expressed in certain paragraphs of the
report concerning the USSR and other socialist countries, in particular
paragraphs 134, 135 and 136. In the world of today characterised by
the existence of quite different socio-economic and legal systems real
account should be taken of the concrete conditions in the countries
when examining questions on the application of Conventions, including
those concerning freedom of association and trade union rights.   In
this perspective, Mr. Ivanov recalled the report of an ILO mission,
"The trade union situation in the USSR", according to which "Another
thing to be remembered is that the structure, functions and rights of
the Soviet trade unions cannot be properly appreciated unless the
economic, political and social structure of the Soviet State is taken
into account. This question of 'background' or national circumstances
is no less important in the case of the Soviet Union than it is in that
of other countries" (page 10).

43. Another member of the Committee, Mr. Gubinski, associating himself with Mr. Ivanov's comments, stated that he did not agree with the Committee's comments on the application of the instruments on freedom of association in several Soviet countries since, in his opinion, account should be taken of the realities of the economic and social systems existing in these countries. He also did not agree with the position taken by the Committee on the question of the dissolution or suspension of workers' and employers' organisations. The report was correct in stating that workers' and employers' organisations should not be subject to dissolution or suspension by administrative authority. This is in conformity with Articles 4 and 6 of Convention No. 87. However, the Committee's position according to which the same principle applies to dissolution or suspension by a law goes beyond the limits of the Convention. Mr. Gubinski does not believe that the Committee may add to the text of a Convention.

44. In the light of the foregoing statements, the Committee wishes to recall the position which it has consistently adopted in examining the extent of implementation of international labour Conventions. The Committee has never ignored the fact that social realities in countries with different social and political systems, even though differing from country to country, may be in conformity with particular ILO Conventions. Divergences between national legislation and practice and such Conventions may, however, occur in countries belonging to any of these systems. In compliance with its terms of reference, while noting the various political, economic and social conditions existing in different countries, the Committee has to examine, and has in fact examined, from a strictly legal point of view to what extent countries give effect in their legislation and practice to the provisions of international labour Conventions, irrespective of their political, social or economic system. The Committee has also, in making this survey, adopted that uniform and objective approach. With respect to the reference made by Mr. Ivanov to the report by an ILO mission on the trade union situation in the USSR, published in 1960, the Committee recalls that the mission in question was called upon to make a factual survey of the situation, but not to assess its compatibility with specific Conventions. As regards the principle relating to the dissolution of trade union organisations, the Committee, having examined the remarks made by Mr. Gubinski, remains convinced that the dissolution or suspension of trade union organisations by legislative means is not in conformity with the purpose of Article 4 of Convention No. 87. It recalls that this view is also in conformity with the principles expressed on this matter by the Committee on Freedom of Association. Finally, the Committee considers that, in any event, the dissolution or suspension of trade union organisations by legislative means would be contrary to Article 8, paragraph 2, of Convention No. 87 under which the law of the land should not be such as to impair, nor shall it be so applied as to impair, the guarantees provided for in the Convention.

Freedom of association

Introduction

45.   The Freedom of Association and Protection of the Right to Organise Convention, 1948 (No. 87) lays down a number of principles for guaranteeing workers and employers free exercise of the right to organise in relation to the public authorities.   The Convention specifies four basic guarantees in this regard. The first is aimed at ensuring that all workers and employers have the right to establish and join organisations of their own choosing without previous authorisation. The second gives the organisations the right to draw up their constitutions and rules, to elect their representatives in full freedom, to organise their administration and activities and to formulate their programmes.   The third protects the organisations against dissolution or suspension by administrative authority.   The fourth grants the organisations the right to establish and join federations and confederations and to affiliate with international organisations of workers and employers. Federations and confederations have the same rights as their affiliated organisations.

46.   To these the Convention adds a further two safeguards: as regards the legal personality of the organisations, federations and confederations, the Convention provides that the acquisition of legal personality may not be made subject to conditions of such a character as to restrict the guarantees mentioned above; as regards respect for the law, in exercising the rights provided for in the Convention workers, employers and their organisations must respect the law of the land but, in return, the law of the land shall not be such as to impair, nor shall it be so applied as to impair, the guarantees provided for in the instrument.

47.   It should also be pointed out that the rights set forth in the Freedom of Association and Protection of the Right to Organise Convention, 1948 (No. 87) are very broadly recognised, inasmuch as they apply to workers and employers alike without distinction whatsoever, and in all branches of activity with the exception of the armed forces and the police. These rights guarantee both to workers and employers the free exercise of the right to organise without interference from the public authorities. Article 10 of the Convention defines the type of organisation envisaged, namely "any organisation of workers or of employers for furthering and defending the interests of workers or of employers".   Article 11 obliges ratifying member States "to take all necessary and appropriate measures to ensure that workers and employers may exercise freely the right to organise". This Article lays down an obligation for the State to take measures to prevent any interference with such rights without qualification, that is interference by individuals, by organisations or by public authorities.

48.   Before examining each of the aspects of freedom of associa- tion covered by Convention No. 87, it is worthwhile to devote a preliminary chapter to a discussion of the relationship between civil liberties and trade union rights inasmuch as the rights and guarantees provided for in the freedom of association Conventions cannot be exercised without respect for basic human rights, since the effective exercise of trade union rights presupposes that civil liberties are guaranteed to citizens.

CHAPTER II

Trade union rights
and civil liberties

49.   The fundamental guarantees of civil liberties are enshrined
in international instruments, in particular, the Universal Declaration
of Human Rights.   Since the Declaration only carries moral force, it
has been expanded and supplemented by two instruments which are binding
upon the States ratifying them: the International Covenant on Economic,
Social and Cultural Rights and the International Covenant on Civil and
Political Rights together with its optional Protocol.   The Covenants
entered into force in 1976.

50.   At the national and regional levels, measures to protect
human rights have been included in numerous national constitutions and
in various regional legal instruments.[1] The international and regional
instruments relating to human rights express general agreement on
certain basic principles which are widely echoed at the national level.
However, the exercise of civil liberties depends not only on formal
rules and institutional provisions but also on the way in which these
rules and provisions are applied in practice, and here various factors
can play an important part (general climate of respect for civil
liberties, detailed legal regulations defining the conditions for
exercising such liberties, effective procedures for guaranteeing
respect for civil liberties, etc.). The body of existing laws and
regulations together with national practice cannot fail to have a
decisive impact on trade union rights. It has been observed, in fact,
that restrictions on freedom of association are more frequently
encountered in cases where civil liberties in general are also
curtailed.[2]

51.   The relationship between civil liberties and trade union
rights has been stressed by the various ILO bodies on numerous
occasions. As far back as 1944, for example, the International Labour
Conference proclaimed, in the Declaration of Philadelphia concerning
the aims and purposes of the International Labour Organisation which is
annexed to the ILO's Constitution, that freedom of expression and of
association are essential to sustained progress and referred to the
fundamental rights which are an inseparable part of human dignity.   In
the preparatory work for Convention No. 87 it was stressed that
"freedom of industrial association is but one aspect of freedom of
association in general, which must itself form part of the whole range
of fundamental liberties of man, all interdependent and complementary
----

[1] For   example,   the   European   Convention   on   Human Rights, 1950;
American Convention on Human Rights, 1969; African Covenant on Human
Rights and the Rights of Peoples, 1981.

[2] See in this respect: ILO, The ILO and human rights, Report of the
Director-General, Part 1, ILC, 52nd Session, Geneva, 1968, p. 36.

one to another, including freedom of assembly and of meeting, freedom of speech and opinion, freedom of expression and of the press, and so forth".[1] In this connection it should be pointed out that the obligation to ensure respect for civil liberties essential to the exercise of trade union rights is implicitly contained in Convention No. 87 since, according to the terms of Article 8, the law of the land shall not be such as to impair, nor shall it be so applied as to impair, the guarantees provided for in the Convention.

52.   More recently, in 1970, the Conference adopted, without opposition, a resolution concerning trade union rights and their relation to civil liberties.[2] Considering, inter alia, "that there exist firmly established, universally recognised principles defining the basic guarantees of civil liberties which should constitute a common standard of achievement for all peoples and all nations", it recognises that "the rights conferred upon workers' and employers' organisations must be based on respect for those civil liberties which have been enunciated in particular in the Universal Declaration of Human Rights and in the International Covenant on Civil and Political Rights and that the absence of these civil liberties removes all meaning from the concept of trade union rights". The Conference explicitly listed the fundamental rights essential for the exercise of freedom of association and in particular: (a) the right to freedom and security of person and freedom from arbitrary arrest and detention; (b) freedom of opinion and expression and in particular freedom to hold opinions without interference and to seek, receive and impart information and ideas through any media and regardless of frontiers; (c) freedom of assembly; (d) the right to a fair trial by an independent and impartial tribunal, and (e) the right to protection of the property of trade union organisations.

53.   Finally, in adopting the Labour Relations (Public Service) Convention, 1978 (No. 151), the Conference referred explicitly to the relationship between the exercise of trade union rights and civil rights since Article 9 in Part VI entitled "Civil and political rights", provides that "public employees shall have, as other workers, the civil and political rights which are essential for the normal exercise of freedom of association".

54.   The supervisory bodies of the ILO - both the Committee on Freedom of Association and the Committee of Experts itself - have also stressed, on a number of occasions, the interdependence between civil liberties and trade union rights. For example, the Committee of Experts noted in its previous general surveys that the degree of freedom enjoyed by occupational organisations in determining and organising their activities depends very largely on certain legislative provisions of general application relating to the right of free meeting, the right of free expression and, in general, to civil and political liberties enjoyed by the inhabitants of the country.[3] Similarly, the opinion has been expressed within the Conference

----

[1] ILO: Freedom of association and industrial relations, Report VII, ILC, 30th Session, 1947, p. 11.

[2] ILO: Record of Proceedings, ILC, 54th Session, 1970, p. 733.

[3] RCE, Report III (Part IV), ILC, 43rd Session, 1959, para. 71, and RCE, General Survey, Report III (Part 4B), ILC, 58th Session, 1973, para. 130.

Committee on the Application of Standards that freedom of association could not really be respected when no other civil liberties were recognised, when the elementary freedom from arbitrary arrest and freedom of the press were not assured and when freedom to meet seemed to be granted only to those trade unions which the government tolerated.[1]

55.   The Committee on Freedom of Association, which has had to deal with a considerable number of cases dealing with the exercise of civil liberties, has stated that a free and independent trade union movement can develop only in a climate of respect for fundamental human rights,[2] and has deemed it useful to stress the importance that should be attached to the fundamental principles enunciated in the Universal Declaration of Human Rights, since violation of these principles may affect the free exercise of trade union rights.[3]

56.   On the basis of the information available and in particular the complaints submitted to the Committee on Freedom of Association, it appears that the main difficulties encountered by trade union organisations and their leaders and members relate to the right to security of the person, freedom of assembly, freedom of opinion and expression, protection of trade union property and premises. Finally, frequent problems also arise with regard to the exercise of trade union rights where the public authorities have decreed states of emergency.

The right to security of the person

57.   The resolution concerning trade union rights and their relation to civil liberties lists as first among the liberties essential for the normal exercise of trade union rights the "right to freedom and security of person and freedom from arbitrary arrest and detention". It is clear that, more than any other, the right to security of the person decisively affects the exercise of trade union rights. The complaints submitted to the Committee on Freedom of Association relate, in particular, to cases of violent death, serious injury, torture, ill-treatment, arbitrary arrest and detention, unjustified internment, exile, restrictions on freedom of movement and summary procedures and disappearances.

Physical assaults against persons

58.   Among the violations of security of persons, physical assaults such as murders, serious injury, ill-treatment and torture constitute particularly serious and irreparable violations of fundamental human rights.

59.   The Committee on Freedom of Association has emphasised that a climate of violence such as that surrounding the murder of trade

----

[1] ILO: Record of Proceedings, ILC, 52nd Session, 1968, Appendix VI, p. 614.

[2] ILO: Committee on Freedom of Association, 211th Report, Cases Nos. 844, 873, 904, 953, 973, 987, 1000 and 1016, para. 430; 213th Report, Cases Nos. 954, 957, 975, 978 and 1026, para. 55.

[3] ILO: Committee on Freedom of Association, 129th Report, Case No. 385, para. 71.

union leaders constitutes a very serious obstacle to the exercise of trade union rights and that such acts require severe measures to be taken by the authorities.[1] Where disorders have occurred involving loss of human life or serious injury, the appointment of an independent commission of inquiry by the government concerned is a particularly appropriate method of ascertaining facts and determining responsibilities.[2]

60. As regards the fate of imprisoned trade unionists, great importance should be attached to the principle laid down in the Universal Declaration of Human Rights and in the International Covenant on Civil and Political Rights according to which all persons deprived of their liberty must be treated with humanity and with respect for the inherent dignity of the human person.[3] Thus, in cases involving allegations relating to the ill-treatment of prisoners, the Committee on Freedom of Association has expressed its strong disapproval of any vexations or brutality inflicted on any prisoners and has considered that complaints concerning ill-treatment of prisoners should be investigated by the government so that the measures which may be called for, including reparation for the injuries inflicted, are taken.[4] In cases containing allegations of torture, the Committee has considered that those responsible for such acts ought to suffer exemplary punishment in order to prevent any recurrence of such practices and that, in addition, the sanctions ought to be accompanied by detailed instructions containing an appropriate warning to those concerned.[5]

Arrest, detention, forced exile and disappearance of persons

61. The arrest and detention of trade unionists constitute particularly serious measures which should be accompanied by all appropriate safeguards, in particular judicial ones. While persons engaged in trade union activities or holding trade union office cannot claim immunity in respect of ordinary criminal law, trade union activities should not in themselves be used by the public authorities as a pretext for the arbitrary arrest, detention or forced exile of trade unionists. The detention or internment of trade unionists, especially trade union leaders, for reasons connected with their activities to defend the interests of workers constitutes a serious violation of civil liberties in general and trade union rights in particular.[6]

----

[1] See, for example, ILO: Committee on Freedom of Association, 217th Report, Case No. 1117, para. 493.

[2] See, for example, ILO: Committee on Freedom of Association, 181st Report, Case No. 833, para. 55.

[3] See in this respect, for example, ILO: Committee on Freedom of Association, 211th Report, Cases Nos. 997, 999 and 1029, para. 486.

[4] See, for example, ILO: Committee on Freedom of Association, 170th Report, Case No. 763, para. 22.

[5] See, for example, ILO: Committee on Freedom of Association, 190th Report, Case No. 899, para. 359.

[6] See in this respect, for example, ILO: Committee on Freedom of Association, 214th Report, Case No. 1097, para. 747.

62.   The Committee on Freedom of Association has emphasised the
right of any person detained or charged to be dealt with in accordance
with normal judicial procedures which should be instituted as rapidly
as possible, fully guarantee his rights of defence and comply with the
provisions of the Internatioal Covenant on Civil and Political Rights.[1]
The prolonged detention of persons before they are brought to trial is
not compatible with the right of all detained persons to a prompt and
fair trial.   The Committee on Freedom of Association has also
emphasised the particular importance that should be attached to the
principle whereby any person who is arrested should be informed at once
of the reasons for his arrest and promptly informed of any charges laid
against him.[2]

63.   Restrictions on the freedom of movement of trade unionists
can constitute serious obstacles to the exercise of trade union rights.
The restriction of a person's movements to a limited area, accompanied
by a prohibition of entry into the area in which his trade union
operates and in which he normally carries on his trade union functions,
is inconsistent with the normal enjoyment of the right of association
and with the exercise of the right to carry on trade union activities
and functions.[3] The same applies to assigning trade unionists to forced
residence thereby depriving them of the possibility of engaging in
trade union activities.

64.   The Committee considers that the forced exile of trade
unionists, in particular trade union leaders, by the public authorities
is a serious measure in that it constitutes not only an infringement of
the human rights and freedom of association of the individuals against
whom such measures are taken, but also because it weakens the trade
union organisations especially when it deprives them of their leaders.
Such measures should be accompanied by all the necessary safeguards and
should not be imposed as a result of the legitimate trade union
activities of the persons concerned.[4]

65.   The Committee has also noted with concern that, in recent
years, the Committee on Freedom of Association has been seized of
numerous cases concerning the disappearance of trade union leaders and
activists.[5] A truly free and independent trade union movement cannot
develop in a climate of violence and uncertainty, and such matters
should be investigated with the utmost care and thoroughness. In
addition, the authorities should take appropriate steps to ensure
effective protection of trade union leaders and activists against such
incidents.
----

[1] See, for example, ILO: Committee on Freedom of Association,
200th Report, Case No. 763, para. 29; 213th Report, Cases Nos. 954,
957, 975 and 1026, para. 58.

[2] See, for example. ILO: Committee on Freedom of Association,
214th Report, Case No. 1054, para. 674.

[3] See, in this respect, for example, ILO: Committee on Freedom of
Association, 114th Report, Cases Nos. 574, 588 and 593, paras. 189 and
190.

[4] See in this respect, for example, ILO: Committee on Freedom of
Association, 217th Report, Case No. 1104, para. 316.

[5] See, for example, ILO: Committee on Freedom of Association,
207th Report, Case No. 823; 210th Report, Case No. 842; 213th and
215th Reports, Cases Nos. 954, 957, 975, 978 and 1026.

Freedom of assembly

66.   Freedom of trade union assembly is obviously an essential
condition for the effective exercise of trade union rights.[1] Special
importance should be attached to the right of trade unions to organise
meetings freely on their own premises, without the need for prior
authorisation or control by the public authorities. Emphasising these
basic principles, the Committee on Freedom of Association has pointed
out that non-interference by governments in the holding and proceedings
of trade union meetings constitutes an essential element of trade union
rights and the public authorities should refrain from any interference
which would restrict this right or impede the lawful exercise thereof.
Article 3, paragraph 2 of Convention No. 87 states that the public
authorities shall refrain from any interference which would restrict
the rights guaranteed in paragraph 1 of that Article or impede the
lawful   exercise thereof.   In so far as the right of assembly
constitutes an element of the right of trade unions to organise their
activities, as specified in paragraph 1 of that Article, inopportune
intervention or arbitrary presence of the public authorities in trade
union meetings is incompatible with the guarantees provided for in the
Convention. Convention No. 87 therefore directly entails respect by
the authorities for certain civil liberties which are essential for the
exercise of trade union rights.

67.   As regards public meetings, demonstrations or processions
on the public highway,[2] the Committee has considered that, although the
right to hold trade union meetings is a basic requisite of freedom of
association, the organisations concerned must observe the general
provisions relating to public meetings, which are applicable to all.
As for restrictions which might be placed upon public meetings and
demonstrations, it rests with the government, which is responsible for
the maintenance of public order, to decide in the exercise of its
corresponding powers whether meetings, including trade union meetings
may, in certain special circumstances, endanger public order and
security and to take the necessary steps. If, in order to avoid
disturbances, the authorities decide to prohibit a meeting in a public
place, they should allow it to be held in some other place where there
would be no fear of disturbances, thereby maintaining the right of
freedom of assembly.[3]

Freedom of opinion and expression

68.   Special importance attaches to the right to express
thoughts freely as an integral part of the freedom which trade union
organisations should enjoy. The right to express opinions through the
press or otherwise is one of the essential elements of trade union

----

[1] As regards freedom of assembly on plantations, see below, para.
353.

[2] ILO: Committee on Freedom of Association: 217th Report, Case No.
1090, para. 104 and Case No. 1125, para. 347.

[3] ILO: Committee on Freedom of Association, 204th Report, Case No.
962, paras. 254 and 255.

rights.[1] This right would be affected by prior censorship of all means of communication and publication of trade union views. Similarly, the application of measures for the control of publications and information may involve a serious interference by the administrative authorities in trade union activities. In such cases the exercise of administrative authority should very rapidly be subject to judicial review.[2]

Protection of trade union premises and property

69.   Infringements of the right to protection of trade union premises and property by the public authorities can take many forms: searches of the headquarters of a trade union or the offices of a trade union newspaper, visits to the private domicile of a trade unionist, the seizure of property and in particular of trade union premises, the closure or sealing up of trade union offices, or the occupation of trade union premises by the police or the army. Regarding more specifically searches of trade union premises, the Committee, while recognising that trade unions, like other associations or persons, cannot claim immunity from such intervention, must emphasise the importance of the principle that such a search should only be made following the issue of a warrant by the ordinary judicial authority where that authority is satisfied that there are reasonable grounds for supposing that evidence exists on the said premises material to a prosecution for a penal offence and on condition that the search should be restricted to the purposes in respect of which the warrant was issued.[3]

70.   Risks of abuse can arise out of a lack of judicial control of searches. While some searches may be justified because there are reliable indications as to the existence of proof of an offence covered by the ordinary penal law, in other cases abuses may occur where the police authorities resort to such measures at their discretion and, for acts which do not constitute offences, do not restore trade union property or keep a trade union office closed.

Trade union rights, civil liberties and state of emergency

71.   Examination of national situations shows that the performance of trade union activities is frequently curtailed or restricted because of the proclamation by the public authorities of a state of emergency. This is becoming more and more frequent and the exercise of trade union rights is seriously endangered thereby. Given the importance of civil liberties in ensuring the effective enjoyment of the guarantees contained in the freedom of association Conventions, the suspension of fundamental rights following the declaration of a state of emergency (state of siege, martial law, etc.) has a direct influence on the application of the Conventions.

----

[1] See in this respect, for example, ILO: Committee on Freedom of Association, 214th Report, Case No. 1021, para. 124.

[2] See in this respect ILO: Committee on Freedom of Association, 131st Report, Case No. 683, para. 201.

[3] See in this respect, for example, ILO: Committee on Freedom of Association, 204th Report, Case No. 856, para. 117.

72.   Here, it should be emphasised that the freedom of association Conventions do not contain any provision permitting derogation from the obligations arising under the Convention, or any suspension of their application, based on a plea that an emergency exists. The Committee considers that, as regards the enjoyment of civil liberties which are essential for the effective exercise of trade union rights, the plea of a state of emergency to justify the restriction of these liberties should only be invoked in circumstances of extreme gravity constituting a case of <u>force majeure</u> and subject to the condition that any measures affecting in any way the guarantees established in the Conventions should be limited both in extent and in time to what is strictly necessary to deal with the particular situation.   The Committee considers that, while it is conceivable that in such situations some civil liberties such as the right of public assembly or the right to hold street demonstrations might be prohibited, it is not permissible, however, that, in the field of trade union activities, the guarantees relating to the security of the person should be abolished, suspended or even limited.

73.   The Committee considers it useful to recall the position of the Commission of Inquiry set up to examine the complaints concerning the observance by Greece of Conventions Nos. 87 and 98, which pointed out that international tribunals and supervisory bodies, when seized of a plea of justification for a state of emergency on such grounds as legitimate self-defence, have invariably made an independent determination as to whether the circumstances justified the claim, and have not allowed the State concerned to be sole judge of the issue.[1]

*

*   *

74.   Firmly established and universally recognised principles define the fundamental guarantees of civil liberties which should constitute the common ideal to be attained by all peoples and all nations; these principles are enunciated in the Universal Declaration of Human Rights and are binding on States which have ratified the international Covenants and in particular the International Covenant on Civil and Political Rights.

75.   The International Labour Organisation, for its part, as well as its supervisory bodies have shown that the enjoyment of the guarantees contained in the pertinent ILO Conventions can only be effective where fundamental civil liberties are recognised and protected, since the exercise of trade union rights depends not only on formal rules and relevant institutional provisions but also on their application in practice.

----

[1] ILO: <u>O.B.</u>, Special Supplement, Vol. LIV, 1971, No. 2, para. 111.

CHAPTER III

Right of workers and employers,
without distinction whatsoever,
to establish organisations

76.   To what extent is the fundamental right of workers and
employers to establish organisations for occupational purposes
recognised in practice? Article 2 of the Freedom of Association and
Protection of the Right to Organise Convention, 1948 (No. 87) lays down
the principle that "Workers and employers, without distinction
whatsoever, shall have the right to establish ... organisations ..."
When it adopted Convention No. 87 by an overwhelming majority, the
International Labour Conference formally acknowledged that the right to
organise was a general right. Convention No. 87 embodied a concept
that had been highlighted in the preparatory work on the instrument,
namely that freedom of association should be guaranteed without
distinction or discrimination of any kind as to occupation, sex,
colour, race, creed, nationality or political opinion.[1] The only
exception to this general principle is that stipulated in Article 9,
which permits States to determine the extent to which the guarantees
provided for in the Convention apply to the armed forces and the
police.

77.   Most countries recognise the right of workers and employers
to organise as provided for in Article 2. In a number of countries,
however, the law draws a distinction as regards the manner in which the
right of association applies to certain occupations or categories of
persons; this distinction may concern large groups of workers such as
public servants, agricultural workers or various other categories such
as domestic workers and seamen, may be dependent on other factors such
as nationality or may refer to the recognition of the right of
association of employers.

Recognition of the right to organise
in the public service

78.   During the preparatory work on Convention No. 87, it was
emphasised that freedom of association should be guaranteed not only to
employers and workers in private industry but also to public
employees.[2] Accordingly, the law and practice report prepared by the
Office provided that public servants and officials should be covered by
the new instrument: "The guarantee of the right of association should
apply to all employers and workers, public or private, and, therefore,
to public servants and officials and to workers in nationalised
----

[1] ILO: Record of Proceedings, ILC, 30th Session, 1947, p. 570.

[2] loc. cit. As regards the scope of Convention No. 98, see para.
255 below.

industries. It has been considered that it would be inequitable to draw any distinction, as regards freedom of association, between wage earners in private industry and officials in the public service, since persons in either category should be permitted to defend their interests by becoming organised. However, the recognition of the right of association of public servants in no way prejudges the question of the right of such officials to strike ...[1]".

79. However, despite the provisions of Article 2, the fact is that, although the legislation of virtually all countries recognises the right of association of workers in the private sector, the same does not always apply to public servants and officials. In some countries, public servants do have exactly the same right of association as workers in the private sector; in others, the right does not exist for certain categories of public servants or is curtailed by restrictions that do not normally apply to other workers. Finally, in some countries, the legislation does not at all recognise the right of public servants and officials to organise.

80. It is not always possible to determine from the law in force in a country the precise extent to which public servants enjoy the right of association in practice. Even in countries where their right to form trade union organisations is not recognised by law, associations, for example, are sometimes set up. These may in fact benefit from the de facto recognition which the government accords them in its capacity as employer for the purpose of discussing wage claims and other aspects of working conditions. Conversely, the fact that the right of association is recognised by law does not necessarily mean that public employees are actually able to establish effective organisations to protect their interests.

Recognition of the principle of the right to organise

81. The right of public servants to organise is often governed by the legislation applying to trade unions in general.[2]

82. In other legislation, the right of public servants to organise is governed by a set of provisions contained in public service statutes or in special legislation.[3]

----

[1] ILO: Freedom of Association and Industrial Relations, Report VII, ILC, 30th Session, 1947, pp. 108-109.

[2] This is the case, for example, in Argentina, Australia, Austria, Benin, Bulgaria, Byelorussian SSR, Central African Republic, Colombia, Costa Rica, Cuba, Cyprus, Czechoslovakia, Denmark, Egypt, Finland, Federal Republic of Germany, France, Greece, Honduras, Hungary, Iceland, India, Ireland, Israel, Italy, Ivory Coast, Kenya, Netherlands, Norway, Philippines, Poland, Portugal, Senegal, Sri Lanka, Swaziland, Sweden, Syrian Arab Republic, Tunisia, Ukrainian SSR, USSR, United Kingdom, Uruguay and Yugoslavia. The Government of Congo states that public servants are considered as workers and there is therefore no specific legislation governing their trade union rights.

[3] For example, Belgium (Act of 19 December 1974), United Republic of Cameroon (Act No. 68-16F-19 and Decree No. 74-138), Canada (Public Service Staff Relations Act, 1970), Djibouti (Order No. 70/553/SG/CD of 14 May 1970), Gabon (Act No. 2/81), Japan (National Public Service Law, 1947, and Local Public Service Law, 1955, as amended), Luxembourg (Act

(Footnote continued on next page)

83.   Sometimes, although the right to organise is not, in
principle, recognised for public servants, certain categories do enjoy
the right by being exempted from the application of the general
legislation.[1]

84.   Moreover public servants can sometimes only form
associations whose activities are limited to cultural and social
matters.[2] Concerning this kind of legislation the Committee would
emphasise that, in accordance with the Convention, public servants have
the right to associate for trade union purposes, and governments should
indicate clearly the kind of trade union activities that may be carried
out by public servants.

(Footnote continued from previous page)

of 1979 establishing the general status of state officials), Mali
(General Public Service Statutes, s. 19; a decree is to be made under
the Statutes for the implementation of this section), Mexico (Federal
Law for Workers in the Service of the State, 1963), New Zealand (State
Services Conditions of Employment Act, 1977; Post Office Act, 1959;
Railways Act, 1981), Peru (Constitution of 1979 and Supreme Decrees
Nos.   003-1982 PCM and 026-82 JUS), Spain (Royal Decrees   Nos.
1522/1977, 3624/1977 and 500/1978), Switzerland (Federal Act respecting
the Conditions of Service of Federal Employees, 1927, s. 13, paragraph
1), Trinidad and Tobago (Civil Service Act No. 29 of 1965 and Education
Act No. 1 of 1966, as amended), United States (Civil Service Reform
Act, 1978; United States Code, Title 5, Chapter 71, and laws in 39
States), Uruguay (Legislative Decree No. 10388 of 1943 concerning the
status of public servants), Venezuela (Trade Unions (Civil Service)
(Regulations) Decree, 1971).

In Guatemala, the Public Service Act, section 63 of which
recognises that servants of the State have the right to associate
freely for occupational purposes, has not been completed by any
provisions for its application.

The Government of Bangladesh states that public employees of
government agencies who are paid through a centralised budget are
entitled to set up and join their own associations.

----

[1] In Malaysia (Trade Unions Act, s. 27(1) and (2)), public
officials do not have the right to join trade unions unless exempted
from this provision by the Yang di-Pertuan Agong (except, however, for
certain categories of officials). The Government states that, under a
Notification of 1981, public officials are allowed to form or be
members of trade unions which confine their membership to a particular
occupation, government department or ministry. However, persons
engaged in a confidential or security capacity are not allowed to do so
while those in the managerial and professional group may do so only if
they are exempted by the Chief Secretary to the Government.

In Singapore, s. 29(a) of the Trade Unions Act prohibits public
employees from joining or becoming members of any trade union unless
the President exempts a given category or class of public employees
from the application of this provision, either completely or under
certain conditions. According to the Government, exemptions have been
granted to all government departments and public bodies other than the
police and armed forces.

[2] Paraguay (Act No. 200/70, s. 31).

Refusal of recognition of the right to organise

85.   At the opposite end of the scale there are countries which refuse, as a matter of principle, to recognise the right of public service officials to organise themselves in trade unions.[1] The application of this principle may be either absolute or partial For example, some legislation prohibits all categories of personnel in the service of the State from forming trade unions; others exclude officials of the state administration; in certain cases the right to organise is even denied to workers in public undertakings[2] and public institutions.[3]

Exclusions and restrictions relating to certain categories of public servants

86.   In cases where the legislation recognises the right of public servants to organise, specific categories in the employ of the State may nevertheless be excluded from doing so or be subjected to certain restrictions in this respect. Such exclusions have often been justified on the grounds that these public servants have special responsibilities or functions.

87.   Among the categories of public servants which are sometimes excluded from the right to establish trade unions are fire service personnel[4] and prison staff,[5] the latter being assimilated in a number of countries, for the purposes of the right to organise, to the police.
----

[1] For example, Bolivia (General Labour Law, 1939, s. 104), Brazil (Consolidated Labour Laws, s. 566), Chad (Ordinance No. 001 of 8 January 1976), Chile (Legislative Decree No. 2756 of 29 June 1979, s. 74), Dominican Republic (Labour Code, s. 3, and Act No. 2059 of 1949), Ecuador (Civil Service and Administrative Career Act, s. 60(g)), El Salvador (Labour Code, s. 2. The Code does however specifically include employees and workers in autonomous and semi-autonomous public institutions), Ethiopia (Labour Proclamation, No. 222 of 1982), Guatemala (Labour Code), Jordan (Labour Act), Liberia (Labour Practices Law, s. 4700), Nicaragua (Labour Code, s. 9; according to the Government, a trade union exists to which public servants and public employees may belong); Yemen (Labour Code, s. 3), Zimbabwe (Law on Conciliation in Labour Matters, Chpt. 267). In Chile, where public servants are denied the right to organise, workers in public undertakings are entitled to establish trade unions (Legislative Decree No. 2756 of 29 June 1979, ss. 1 and 74).

[2] For example, Liberia (Labour Practices Law, s. 4700).

[3] For example, Brazil (Consolidated Labour Laws, s. 566). However, the Committee was able to note with satisfaction in 1977 the adoption of Act No. 6128 dated 6 November 1974 which gives formal recognition to the right of unionisation of employees of semi-public undertakings.

[4] For example, in Gabon, Japan, Sudan.

[5] For example, in Colombia, Gabon, Japan, Malaysia, Mexico, Nigeria, Pakistan, Poland, Sri Lanka, Sudan, Swaziland, Tanzania, Zambia and Zimbabwe. In Trinidad and Tobago and Uganda, special statutes dealing with the conditions of employment of this category of personnel provide that the workers concerned may form government-approved staff associations, although such associations cannot be registered as trade unions.

In the Committee's view, the functions exercised by these categories of public servants would not normally justify their exclusion from the right to organise, on the basis of Article 9 of the Convention.

88.   Finally, in certain countries the legislation imposes special restrictions on the right of association of public servants employed at the higher levels of the administration and some of their supporting staff, that is, public servants occupying managerial or supervisory positions of trust.[1] However, this does not always exclude their right to group together in organisations. In a certain number of cases, for example, these categories of public servants seem to have the right to form associations to protect their occupational interests, provided they do not join associations of public employees of a lower grade. (The question here is more one of affiliation than of recognition of the right to organise itself.[2]) The Committee considers that these categories should be entitled to establish their own organisations and that, where association with other public servants is not allowed, the legislation should limit this category to persons exercising important managerial or policy-making responsibilities.

89.   The armed forces and the police are the only categories which, in accordance with the Convention, may be excluded from the benefits of its provisions. In fact, the point is often made that the armed forces and police are responsible for the external and internal security of the State. Members of the armed forces are in fact the category of public servants most frequently denied the right to organise, although certain legal systems allow them to group together to defend their occupational interests - sometimes, however, with

----

[1] This is the case, for example, in Colombia, Egypt, Gabon, Mexico, Nigeria, Peru, Singapore, Sri Lanka.

In Gabon, Act No. 2/81 denies court magistrates the right to organise and allows provision for special restrictions in the case of officials with specific responsibilities.

In Mexico, where public officials occupying confidential posts are excluded from the Federal Law for Workers in the Service of the State, the posts concerned are clearly specified: the list includes directors, assistant directors, chiefs and assistant chiefs of department, office and section, inspectors, technical staff, legal and technical advisers, labour disputes conciliators, school directors, auditors, treasurers, supervisors and administrators of various types and certain secretarial positions.

In Nigeria, Decree No. 31 of 1973 excludes the following from the right to form trade unions: customs employees, employees of the mint, of the Central Bank and of the External Telecommunications Company.

In Peru, Supreme Decree No. 003-82 PCM, ss. 2 and 3, excludes in particular court magistrates and officials having the power of decision or occupying confidential posts.

In Singapore, public servants who hold appointments in the managerial grade may, as a condition of appointment, transfer or promotion, be required to resign from trade union membership (s. 77 of the Industrial Relations Act).

[2] See below, para. 130.

certain specific restrictions.[1] Members of the police and security forces are also frequently denied the right to organise. Countries which deny this right to members of the armed forces often include the police under the same heading and generally apply the same legislative provisions in both cases. Sometimes, though not allowed to become members of a trade union, members of the police are entitled to create and join their own associations.[2] On the other hand, there are countries where the police have the same right to organise as other categories of public servants or are entitled to do so under separate legislation.[3]

The right to organise of agri-
cultural workers

90.   The agricultural sector is another branch where workers frequently encounter obstacles - whether of a _de jure_ or _de facto_ nature - to their organisation in trade unions. These problems will be examined in greater detail in Chapter XIII, which deals with the application of the Rural Workers' Organisations Convention (No. 141) and Recommendation (No. 149), 1975.

Recognition of the right to organise of
certain other categories of workers

91.   Certain other categories of workers are also sometimes denied the right to form trade unions. The Committee has, for example, been called upon to examine the right to organise of domestic staff, persons working at home and in family workshops, persons working in charitable institutions,[4] seamen, executive and managerial staff, etc.[5]

----

[1] For example, in Austria, Denmark, Finland, Federal Republic of Germany, Luxembourg, Norway, Sweden, United Kingdom.

[2] Provisions for their joint exclusion are to be found in Malaysia, Mexico and Morocco.

[3] For example, in Australia, Austria, Belgium, Denmark, Finland, France, Federal Republic of Germany, Guinea, Iceland, Ireland, Ivory Coast, Luxembourg, Malawi, Netherlands, New Zealand, Niger, Norway, Senegal, Sweden, Tunisia, United Kingdom.

[4] In the case of the Philippines, the Committee noted with satisfaction in 1981 the promulgation of Act No. 386 of 1 May 1980 extending the right to organise for purposes of collective bargaining to persons employed in non-profit, religious, charitable, medical or educational institutions. In addition, it noted with interest that under the same legislation ambulant, temporary and itinerant workers, self-employed people, rural workers and those without any definite employers may form labour organisations for the purpose of advancing and defending their interests and for their mutual aid and protection (s. 244 of the Labour Code) (RCE 1981, p. 119).

[5] The Committee has questioned certain States with regard to the right of these various categories of workers to form trade unions, for example: Bangladesh (denial of the right to organise to persons employed in managerial or administrative posts); Bolivia (denial of the right to organise to home workers, domestic staff and temporary workers); Greece (exclusion of seamen from the general provisions relating to occupational organisations); Madagascar (right to organise

(Footnote continued on next page)

Depending on the country's legislation the last-named category may be denied the right to organise or may be entitled to do so provided they do not combine with employees of a lower grade.

92.   Since they are not specifically excluded from Convention No. 87, all these categories of workers should naturally be covered by the guarantees afforded by the Convention and should, in particular, have the right to establish and join organisations.

Other aspects of the recognition of the right to organise: restrictions based on race, nationality, sex, political opinions

93.   Problems of recognition of the right to organise may also stem from restrictions relating, for example, to race, nationality, sex, opinion and political affiliation. In countries where they exist, restrictions of this nature may affect the right to organise itself or concern more specifically the question of membership.

Race

94.   During the preparatory work on Convention No. 87, it was made quite clear that the right of workers to establish organisations should be guaranteed "without discrimination as to race".

95.   Racial distinctions do not normally appear in national legislation. In some countries it may actually be explicitly prohibited by law, with, for example, a stipulation that no employee may be denied union membership on grounds of race.[1] In others it is unlawful for a trade union to discriminate against a member by refusing or deliberately omitting to accord him the same benefits as are accorded to other members.[2] Some laws relating to human rights and fair labour practices prohibit any form of racial discrimination in trade union membership.[3] It may also be unlawful for a union to limit, segregate or classify its membership according to race, colour or national origin.[4] At the opposite extreme, any legislation that imposes a system of racial discrimination with regard to the right of workers to establish and join trade unions of their own choosing is in blatant violation of the Convention.[5]

(Footnote continued from previous page)

of seamen); Nicaragua (right to organise of persons working in family workshops and self-employed persons in the urban and rural sectors); Peru (denial of the right to organise to workers in welfare societies, hospitals and similar branches).

[1] For example, in Argentina (Act No. 22105 of 1979, s. 7); El Salvador (Labour Code, s. 204); Japan (Trade Union Law No. 174, 1949, s. 5).

[2] United Kingdom (Race Relations Act, 1976, s. 11).

[3] Canada.

[4] United States (Civil Rights Act).

[5] With regard to the union situation in the Republic of South Africa, see, in particular, the Declaration concerning the Policy of Apartheid in South Africa, adopted by the Conference at its 67th
(Footnote continued on next page)

Nationality

96.   Restrictions on the right to organise based on nationality
exist in varying degrees in national legislations. In some countries
citizenship is a condition of trade union membership;[1]   in others a
certain proportion of the members must be nationals or citizens;[2] in
yet others trade union affiliation of non-nationals is subject to
conditions of residence or reciprocity.[3]

97.   Restrictions based on nationality may, in particular,
prevent migrant workers from playing an active role in the defence of
their interests, especially in sectors where they are the major source
of labour. The ILC has given its attention to this aspect of migrants'
working conditions in some of the legal standards that it has adopted.
Article 6, paragraph 1(a)(ii), of the Migration for Employment Convention (Revised), 1949 (No. 97), states that equal treatment must be
applied in respect of membership of trade unions and enjoyment of the
benefits of collective bargaining. Article 10 of the Migrant Workers
(Supplementary Provisions) Convention, 1975 (No. 143), provides that
the principle of equality of opportunity and treatment must apply to
trade union rights. These rights are set out in greater detail in
Paragraph 2(g) of the Migrant Workers Recommendation, 1975 (No. 151),
which refers to membership of trade unions, exercise of trade union
rights and eligibility for office in trade unions and in labour-
management relations bodies, including bodies representing workers in
undertakings.

(Footnote continued from previous page)

Session (1981) (Record of Proceedings, ILC, 67th Session, 1981, No. 19,
pp. 14-17) and the Special Report of the Director-General on the
Application of the Declaration concerning the Policy of Apartheid in
South Africa (ILC, 68th Session, 1982), as well as the Report of the
Committee on Apartheid (Record of Proceedings, ILC, 68th Session, 1982,
No. 22).

[1] For example, Libyan Arab Jamahiriya (the Workers' Trade Unions
Act No. 107, 1975, restricts membership to Arab workers;   non-Arab
workers may however join trade unions in accordance with conditions to
be laid down by the Minister of Labour and Public Service, in agreement
with the Workers' Trade Union Federation); Philippines (Labour Code, s.
270); Togo (Labour Code, s. 6).

[2] For example, Colombia (two-thirds of the membership, Labour Code,
s. 384); Panama (75 per cent of the membership, Labour Code, s. 347).

In the case of Honduras, the Committee noted with satisfaction in
1980 that Decree No. 760 of 25 May 1979 put an end to the requirement
that at least 90 per cent of the members of a trade union should be
citizens of Honduras.

[3] For example, Central African Republic (residence of at least two
years, Labour Code, s. 6); Syrian Arab Republic (non-Arab workers
employed in the Syrian Arab Republic for more than one year, Decree No.
84 of 1968, s. 25). In Kuwait, reciprocity is not a requirement but
foreign workers can join a trade union only if they have a work permit
and five consecutive years of residence in the country (Ordinance No.
38 of 1964).

Sex and age

98.   Trade union legislation normally makes no distinction based on sex; some countries even include provisions which implicitly or explicitly prohibit any discrimination in this respect.[1] In several countries, where restrictions on the right to organise might result from provisions contained in the Civil Code, trade union legislation provides specifically that a married women may join a trade union without the authorisation of her husband.[2] Certain countries have legislative provisions concerning union membership of minors.[3]

Political affiliation or activities

99.   Few references exist in national legislation to the political opinions or affiliation of individuals as a criterion for recognition of their right to organise. In some cases, the law seeks to prevent any discrimination by trade unions against their members on grounds of political beliefs.[4] In some other cases, however, the right of association may be restricted by law by reason for a person's supposedly subversive opinions or activities or membership of particular organisations. In one country, no occupational organisation may knowingly admit as a member or allow to continue in membership any individual who belongs to a subversive organisation or is engaged directly or indirectly in a subversive activity or movement.[5] In another country, persons professing subversive political opinions forfeit all rights of association.[6]

100.   The Committee considers that any measure taken under a country's legislation whereby an individual is deprived of his right to become or remain a trade union member for professing certain political opinions or engaging in certain legitimate political activities in a

----

[1] For example, United Republic of Cameroon (Labour Code, s. 1); Central African Republic (Labour Code, s. 1); United States (Civil Rights Act, s. 703); Venezuela (Labour Code, 1947, s. 165).

[2] This is the case of France (Labour Code, Book IV, s. L.411-5). Similar provisions exist in Benin (Labour Code, s. 10); Chad (Labour Code, s. 43); Congo (Labour Code, s. 185); Guinea (Labour Code, s. 9); Haiti (Labour Code, s. 269); Ivory Coast (Labour Code, s. 7); Mali (Labour Code, s. 285); Mauritania (Labour Code, Book III, s. 5); Morocco (Dahir No. 1-57-119, s. 5); Niger (Labour Code, s. 7); Rwanda (Labour Code, s. 9); Senegal (Labour Code, s. 8).

Provisions to this effect have also been adopted in Bolivia (Decree of 23 August 1943, s. 122) and Chile (Legislative Decree No. 2756 of 29 June 1979, which stipulates that women are eligible for election to the administration and management of trade unions).

[3] For example, Congo (Labour Code, s. 189); Togo (Labour Code, s. 7, which provides that minors over the age of 16 may belong to a trade union unless an objection is raised by their father, mother or guardian). Similar provisions exist in Tunisia.

[4] For example, Argentina (Act No. 22105, 1979, s. 7).

[5] Philippines (Labour Code, s. 242).

[6] Turkey (Act No. 5844, 1951, to amend the Penal Code).

manner unconnected with his participation in an occupational organisation would constitute an infringement of the right to organise as it is recognised in Article 2 of the Convention. Conviction for a political offence should in no case constitute a valid ground for withdrawal of trade union membership.

101. As the Committee on Freedom of Association has stated, workers should have the right, without any discrimination of any kind on the basis of political opinion, to join the union of their choice.[1]

Employers

102. As the Committee has already pointed out,[2] Convention No. 87 covers employers as well as workers. Provisions governing the right to organise are normally the same for both. In certain countries, however, employers are excluded from the general trade union law;[3] in others, they are governed by special regulations.[4] A distinction must be drawn between countries where private employers exist and those where, under the prevailing system, there is little or no private enterprise. In the second group of countries the right to organise acquires an additional significance for those who are responsible for the direction and management of the undertakings, since the rights and guarantees laid down in Convention No. 87 must be secured for all workers and employers, including the managers of enterprises belonging to the State.[5]

*
* *

103. The guarantees of Convention No. 87 should apply to all workers and employers, without any distinction. It is apparent from the foregoing analysis, however, that national legislations restrict the recognition of the right to organise in varying degrees, particularly in respect of certain categories of workers such as public servants, managerial staff, non-nationals and agricultural workers. Restrictions of this nature are contrary to the explicit provisions of the Convention.

----

[1] Committee on Freedom of Association, 187th Report, Case No. 857, para. 268.

[2] See para. 77 above.

[3] For example, in Argentina, Egypt, Liberia and Uganda.

[4] For example, Portugal (Legislative Decree No. 215-C/75 of 30 April 1975); Zaire (Act No. 72-028 of 27 July 1972); Zambia (Industrial Relations Act, 1971, Part V).

[5] See RCE, General Survey, Report III (Part 4B), 1973, para. 49.

CHAPTER IV

The right of workers and employers
to establish organisations
without previous authorisation

104. According to Article 2 of Convention No. 87, workers and employers have the right to establish organisations "without previous authorisation".

105. The Convention thus guarantees to the founders of a trade union the right to establish their organisation without the public authorities being able to require them to obtain previous authorisation. It is in the light of this principle that the more or less detailed formalities which are usually prescribed by law for the establishment of an occupational organisation have to be considered. In the preparatory work on the Convention,[1] it was stated that countries would remain free to provide such formalities in their legislation as appeared appropriate to ensure the normal functioning of industrial organisations. It follows, therefore, that the formalities imposed by national regulations concerning the constitution and operation of workers' and employers' organisations are not in themselves incompatible with the provisions of the Convention, provided of course that they do not impair the guarantees granted by the Convention, that they are not tantamount to a "previous authorisation" that would be contrary to Article 2 of the Convention and that they do not create an obstacle which amounts in practice to prohibition.

106. Since the matter of formal requirements for establishing an organisation is closely bound up with that of legal recognition, the legislation of many countries makes the acquisition of legal personality a substantive condition of its existence and activities. Article 7 of Convention No. 87 lays down specifically that the acquisition of legal personality by workers' and employers' organisations "shall not be made subject to conditions of such character as to restrict the application of the provisions of Articles 2, 3 and 4" of the Convention, in other words the right to establish organisations freely.

107. As to the formalities themselves and the form they may take, certain countries do not stipulate any requirement for the establishment of an organisation,[2] which may then either have no legal personality or acquire it automatically.

----

[1] ILO: Record of Proceedings, ILC, 31st Session, 1948, First Report of the Committee on Freedom of Association and Industrial Relations, p. 477.

[2] For example, Belgium, Denmark, Federal Republic of Germany, Iceland, Italy, Luxembourg, Norway, Sweden and Switzerland.

108. In most countries, however, certain formalities such as depositing rules[1] or registering the occupational organisation have to be fulfilled at the time of its establishment.

Filing an organisation's rules

109. The legislation of a number of countries provides that an organisation must deposit its rules,[2] sometimes together with the names of its officers. This requirement is not a prior condition for the granting of an authorisation by the public authorities but merely a formality to ensure that a union's rules are made public, although sometimes the authorities will request the officers of the organisation to amend any clause of the rules which might be contrary to the law. The filing of an organisation's by-laws often confers legal personality on the organisation.

Registration

110. In a great many countries organisations are required to register with a judicial body or with a registrar or with the relevant administrative authority (Ministry of Labour, etc.). Though normally compulsory, registration may also be optional. Depending on the case it may be a mere formality, similar to the filing of the organisation's rules, or be subject to more or less stringent conditions.

111. Certain legal systems stipulate that registration is optional,[3] but organisations which do register gain a number of important advantages, such as special immunities, tax exemptions, the right to have recourse to the dispute settlement machinery or to the procedure for dealing with unfair labour practices, or the right to obtain recognition as exclusive bargaining agent on behalf of a given category of workers. A trade union which chooses to register has to fulfil certain formalities, such as filing information relating to the establishment of the organisation and depositing its rules. Such

---

[1] As for the contents of rules, in particular the question of model rules, see under Chapter VI.

[2] For example, Benin (Labour Code, s. 8); Central African Republic (Labour Code, s. 7); Chad (Labour Code, s. 8); France (Labour Code, Book IV, s. L.411-3); Guinea (Labour Code, s. 6); Israel (Act on Societies, s. 6); Ivory Coast (Labour Code, s. 5); Madagascar (Labour Code, s. 5); Mali (Labour Code, s. 283), Morocco (Dahir No. 1-57-119, s. 3); Niger (Labour Code, s. 5); Portugal (Decrees Nos. 215-B/75 and 215-C/75); Senegal (Labour Code, s. 6); Spain (Act No. 19/1977 and Decree No. 873/1977); United States (for workers' organisations only; detailed information must also be supplied on such matters as financial management, contributions, meetings, etc. Labour-Management Reporting and Disclosure Act, 1959). Provisions concerning the deposit of trade union rules also exist or apply in the French non-metropolitan territories.

[3] For example, in Australia (Commonwealth Conciliation and Arbitration Act, State Trade Union Acts and Arbitration Act); India (Trade Union Act, 1926, as amended); Japan (Trade Union Law, 1949, and Law No. 80 of 21 June 1978); New Zealand (Industrial Relations Act, ss. 163 and 168); Pakistan (Industrial Relations Ordinance, 1969, as amended); Philippines (Labour Code, s. 243).

provisions do not normally pose any problem as regards the requirements of the Convention. However, where under a system of optional registration an organisation has to register in order to secure certain fundamental rights so as to be able to defend and further the interests of its members, the mere fact of the relevant authority having discretionary power to refuse registration would create a situation akin to that in which previous authorisation is required.[1]

112. Registration in numerous countries is _compulsory_ and is a prerequisite for the normal functioning of an organisation.[2]

113. Sometimes the registration procedure, like the filing of union rules, is a mere formality. The organisation must submit its rules and certain other information relating to its officers and founder members, and registration is granted when the authorities are satisfied that the organisation has complied with the provisions of the trade union legislation. In these cases, it is important that organisations are able to appeal against refusal to the judicial authorities. Generally speaking, registration confers legal personality on the organisation.[3]

----

[1] For example, in Western Australia registration of a society may be refused if it is not necessary or desirable for, or would not be likely to advance, the purposes and objectives of the law (Industrial Arbitration Act, 1979, s. 55(4)). In New Zealand, the Registrar of Industrial Unions may refuse to register any society as a union if, in his opinion, the members might conveniently belong to an existing union. If the society is dissatisfied with this decision, it may appeal to the Arbitration Court, and must prove that it would not be more convenient for its members to belong to the existing union (Industrial Relations Act, 1973, s. 168).

[2] This is the case, for example, in Argentina (Act No. 22105, s. 27); Bahamas (Industrial Relations Act, s. 6); Bolivia (General Labour Act and Decree made under the Act, ss. 99 and 124); Brazil (Consolidated Labour Laws, s. 558); United Republic of Cameroon (Labour Code, s. 6); Costa Rica (Labour Code, s. 274); Cyprus (Trade Unions Law, 1965, ss. 7 and 17); Ecuador (Labour Code, ss. 438-440, 441 and 455); Ethiopia (Proclamation No. 222, 1982, s. 17); Gabon (Labour Code, s. 174); Ghana (Trade Unions Ordinance, 1941, ss. 10-12); Greece (Act No. 1264/1982, s. 2 and Civil Code, ss. 79 and 83; Guatemala (Labour Code, ss. 217 and 218); Haiti (Labour Code, s. 268); Jamaica (Trade Union Law, ss. 6 and 13); Kenya (Trade Unions Ordinance, 1952, s. 9, and new Industrial Relations Charter, 1980); Lebanon (Labour Code); Libyan Arab Jamahiriya (Trade Unions Act, 1975, ss. 6-10); Malawi (Trade Union Ordinance, s. 11); Malaysia (Trade Unions Act, s. 8); Malta (Industrial Relations Act, 1976, ss. 2, 9, 15 and 21); Mexico (Federal Labour Law, ss. 365 and 366); Nigeria (Decree No. 31/1973, s. 2); Poland (Trade Union Law, 1982, s. 19); Sierra Leone (Trade Unions Act, s. 9); Singapore (Trade Unions Act, ss. 8 and 19); Tanzania (Trade Unions Ordinance, ss. 7-18); Venezuela (Labour Code, s. 179, and Decree No. 1563/73); Zaire (Labour Code, s. 231); Zambia (Industrial Relations Act, 1971, s. 6). Registration is also compulsory in the non-metropolitan territories of the United Kingdom.

[3] In the case of _Japan_, the Committee noted with _satisfaction_ in 1979 that Act No. 80 of 21 June 1978 provides for the registration of trade unions in the public sector with the competent authorities and that the registration certificate confers legal personality on the unions concerned.

114. In other countries the law confers on the relevant authorities more or less discretionary powers in deciding whether or not an organisation is qualified for registration, thus creating a situation which is similar to that in which "previous authorisation" is required.[1] On this point the Committee on Freedom of Association has observed that the formalities prescribed by legislation should not be of such nature as to hamper freedom to form trade unions nor be applied in such a way as to delay or prevent the setting up of occupational organisations.[2] Consequently, provisions subjecting the right to form an organisation to the obtainment of an authorisation whose issue is at the sole discretion of the authority and provisions granting the authority discretionary powers in approving the rules of an organisation are incompatible with the Convention.

115. With regard to the discretionary powers conferred on administrative authorities in reaching their decision on the activities or presumed objects of an organisation seeking registration, the Committee considers that, in order to obviate any risk of abuse, supervision of the trade union activities should normally be carried out a posteriori and the decision of the administrative authority should be subject to judicial review. The administrative authorities should not be able to refuse registration of an organisation simply because they consider that the organisation could exceed normal union activities, or that it might not be in a position to exercise its functions. Such a system would be tantamount to subjecting the compulsory registration of trade unions to the previous authorisation of the administrative authorities.

116. Similar situations arise when the registration procedure is long and complicated, when registration regulations are applied in a manner inconsistent with their purpose or when the competent administrative authorities make excessive use of broad discretionary powers given to them and are encouraged to do so by the imprecision of the relevant legislation. These factors can be a serious obstacle to the establishment of a trade union and lead to a denial of the right to organise without previous authorisation. Legislation should clearly define the precise conditions that trade unions have to fulfil in order

----

[1] In Gabon, for example, a trade union seeking registration must submit the certificate of affiliation to the Sole Trade Union Confederation with its request (Labour Code, s. 174). In Ghana, registration is granted if the Registrar is of the opinion that any objections brought to his notice are not of sufficient substance to justify a refusal (Trade Unions Ordinance, s. 11). In Kenya, the Registrar must, before approving the establishment of a trade union, seek the opinion of the COTU and FKE (sole federations of workers and employers); the Minister of Labour must be personally consulted and endorses the recommendations of the Permanent Secretary of Labour to the Registrar (Industrial Relations Charter, 1980). In Malaysia, the Registrar must refuse to register a trade union if he considers that it is likely to be used for unlawful purposes or purposes inconsistent with its rules (Trade Unions Act, s. 12(2)). In Singapore and Zimbabwe the Registrar may refuse registration on the same grounds. He may also refuse if he considers that a trade union is liable to be used against the interests of the workers concerned (Trade Unions Act, s. 10 and Law on Conciliation in Labour Matters, s. 41, respectively).

[2] See, for example, ILO: Committee on Freedom of Association, 177th Report, Case No. 889, para. 332, and 199th Report, Case No. 891, para. 74.

to be registered or for a registrar to refuse or cancel registration and should contain explicit criteria for determining whether or not an organisation meets the conditions.

Appeal to the courts

117. Generally speaking, trade unions should have the right to appeal to independent courts against any administrative decision regarding their registration, as a necessary safeguard against unlawful or ill-founded decisions by the authorities responsible for registering trade unions.[1] Although this right seems to exist in many countries the appeal can sometimes be lodged only with the competent minister or another labour authority.[2] An appeal of this nature is liable to lack the necessary conditions of objectivity. Nor would the existence of a procedure of appeal to a court seem to provide sufficient guarantees since it does not alter the nature of the powers conferred on the registration authorities. The judges hearing an appeal should be able to ensure not only that the legislation has been correctly applied; they should also be able to re-examine the substance of a case as well as the grounds on which an administrative decision was taken.

118. The Committee has already indicated in previous General Surveys that, in a certain number of countries, the prior control of the State may be exercised through the legislation relating to public and private meetings. In so far as the holding of meetings to constitute an organisation requires, like any other meeting, previous authorisation by the government or administrative authorities, such meetings may depend in fact, as well as in law, on the consent of the competent authorities.[3]

* * *

119. The right of workers and employers to establish organisations "without previous authorisation", under the terms of Article 2 of the Convention, does not necessarily mean that they should have complete freedom in this respect. Although some countries impose no legal requirements, others require organisations to observe certain formalities; these are often designed to make the establishment of the organisation public and involving the filing of rules or registration with a competent authority. When the authorities are given discretionary powers in the matter, however, there is a danger of abuse

----

[1] See, for example, ILO: Committee on Freedom of Association, 168th Report, Cases Nos. 825 and 849, para. 148.

[2] For example, Bahamas (Industrial Relations Act, s. 13); Malaysia (Trade Unions Act, s. 71A); Singapore (Trade Unions Act, ss. 17 and 18); Swaziland (Industrial Relations Act, s. 24).

[3] The Committee has referred to the situation in the Byelorussian SSR, the Ukrainian SSR and the USSR, in relation to the Decree of 15 May 1935 respecting the procedure for convening congresses (general assemblies, conferences and meetings). In connection with this Decree, the Committee had taken note of the statement made by a Government representative to the Conference Committee in 1960, according to which the provisions in question have never been applied in practice to occupational organisations, and are considered as being in desuetude as regards other social organisations.

and of a situation arising that is tantamount to a requirement of previous authorisation. Provisions of this nature are therefore incompatible with Convention No. 87. The possibility of appealing to the courts against any administrative decision of this kind should in any case exist so that they can examine the substance of the case as well as the grounds or which the decision was taken.

CHAPTER V

The right of workers and employers
to establish and join organisations
of their own choosing

120. Under the terms of Article 2 of Convention No. 87, workers and employers have the right "to establish and, subject only to the rules of the organisation concerned, to join organisations of their own choosing". Recognition of this right is one of the most important principles enshrined in the Convention.

121. The free exercise of this right implies free determination of the structure and membership of trade unions. In many countries, however, this right is subjected to restrictive legal provisions, giving rise to several problems concerning freedom in choosing the structure and composition of organisations and the question of trade union unity or pluralism.

Structure and composition

122. In many countries, the right of workers and employers to organise freely is subject to legal or statutory restrictions, some of which may be incompatible with Article 2 of the Convention. In particular, this may be the case where questions arise concerning the minimum number of persons or the restriction of membership to the occupation or branch of activity covered by the trade union, or to certain categories of workers (public employees, managerial staff and agricultural workers[1] among others).

Minimum number of members

123. In some countries there are no legislative provisions regarding the number of members necessary for establishing an organisation. In many others, however, an organisation may not be established unless it has a minimum number of members. This number varies from one country to another. It ought to be limited to a reasonable figure so that the establishment of organisations is not hindered.[2]

----

[1] On this last point, see Chapter XIII below.

[2] See, for example, Kuwait (Labour Law, 1964, s. 71); Nigeria (Decree No. 22/1978); Panama (Labour Code, s. 344); Uganda (Trade Unions Decree, 1976, s. 8); Western Australia (Industrial Arbitration Act, 1979, s. 53(1) requires membership of at least 200 workers; under the terms of s. 53(2), any association with a smaller membership may be registered if the number of its members constitutes a substantial proportion of all workers in the industry concerned, or if there is good reason, in conformity with the objectives of the Act, to allow registration. At the federal level, the Conciliation and Arbitration

(Footnote continued on next page)

124. The same problems arise when the legislation stipulates that an organisation may only be set up if it has 50 members in the same occupation or undertaking[1] or if it requires a high minimum proportion (sometimes even more than 50 per cent) of workers, which, in this latter case, in fact precludes the establishment of more than one trade union in each occupation or undertaking.[2]

Membership limited to workers of the same occupation or branch of activity

125. Some legal systems stipulate that members of a trade union must belong to the same or similar trade, activities or occupation. Other legal systems provide that the law shall fix the structure, by occupation or branch of activity, of the trade union movement.[3] Where such provisions apply to first-level organisations these organisations must be free to join federations and confederations in the form and manner deemed most appropriate by the workers or employers concerned.[4]

Public servants

126. The Committee has pointed out[5] that the guarantees contained in Convention No. 87, and in particular recognition of the right of association, apply to workers in the public sector as well as those in the private sector. While some legal systems do not recognise the right of civil servants and state employees to associate, others, although allowing the formation of trade unions, impose restrictions on union membership. This is the case when the law forbids public employees to establish joint trade unions comprising both public and private sector employees.[6] It is admissible for first-level organisations of public servants to be limited to that category of
----
(Footnote continued from previous page)

Act, 1904, requires a minimum membership of 100 persons for the registration of a trade union).

[1] For example, Syrian Arab Republic (Legislative Decree No. 84, ss. 2 and 8).

[2] For example, Nicaragua (absolute majority of workers in the undertaking, Labour Code, s. 189); Philippines (30 per cent of the employees in the bargaining unit, Labour Code, s. 234(c)).

See also, para. 133 below.

In Portugal, the law stipulates a minimum membership of 10 per cent or 2,000 workers. The Attorney-General of the Republic has declared the provision in question unconstitutional.

[3] For example, Iraq (Labour Law No. 151, s. 127); Jordan (Labour Code, ss. 69 and 84); Libyan Arab Jamahiriya (Act No. 107/75, ss. 1 and 2); Sudan (Employees' Trade Unions Act, 1977, s. 9).

[4] On this point see below, paras. 242 to 245.

[5] See above, para. 78.

[6] Malaysia (Trade Unions Act, s. 27).

workers, on condition, however, that their organisations are not also restricted to employees of any particular ministry, department or service, and that the first-level organisations, like those of workers in the private sector, may freely join the federations and confederations of their own choosing.[1] Provisions stipulating that different organisations must be established for each category of public servants are incompatible with the right of workers to establish and join organisations of their own choosing.[2]

Managerial staff

127. The right to organise poses special problems for managerial and supervisory staff and employees occupying posts of confidence, both in the private and in the public sector.

128. In some cases there are provisions prohibiting these persons from joining or belonging to trade unions which are open to lower-grade employees or expressly forbidding managerial staff to join workers' unions.[3]

129. In other cases, instead of directly prohibiting managerial and supervisory staff from forming organisations together with general employees, the law denies workers' unions the right to represent managerial staff.[4] Furthermore, in some countries the law provides that an employer may require a person, upon his appointment or promotion to a managerial position, to cease to be, or not to become, an officer or member of a workers' union.[5]

130. Like those of the private sector, senior or middle-grade managerial staff in the public sector are sometimes denied the possibility of associating with other categories of employees in trade union organisations. In some cases, the laws governing the public sector clearly define the groups thus affected. In others, the

----

[1] As regards Cyprus, the Committee noted with satisfaction in 1981 that section 59(1) of the Public Service Law, expressly forbidding public servants to join trade unions which were not limited to the public sector, was repealed by Law No. 31 of 1980.

[2] For example, Malaysia (Trade Unions Act, s. 27); Mexico (Federal Law for Workers in the Service of the State); Sri Lanka (Trade Unions Act).

In Malaysia, workers employed in a statutory authority may only join trade unions limited to persons employed in that establishment, and trade unions which are established in this way may not affiliate to another trade union or a federation which is not limited in this way (Trade Unions Act, s. 27(3)(a) and (b)).

[3] For example, Guatemala (Labour Code, s. 212); Japan (Trade Union Law, s. 2); Mexico (Federal Labour Law, s. 363); Philippines (Labour Code, ss. 245 and 246).

[4] For example, Malaysia (Industrial Relations Act); Singapore (Industrial Relations Act).

[5] For example, Malaysia (Industrial Relations Act, s. 5); Pakistan (Industrial Relations Ordinance, s. 15); Singapore (Industrial Relations Act, s. 78).

categories of staff to be excluded must be agreed upon by the public employer and the trade unions. In still other cases, the government authorities are empowered to determine unilaterally which employees are to be defined as managerial staff.[1]

131. It is generally claimed that such provisions are designed to prevent interference by employers in trade union activities and to avoid conflicts of interest involving managerial staff. Forbidding these persons to join trade unions representing other workers is not necessarily incompatible with freedom of association, but only on two conditions: first, that they have the right to form their own organisations to defend their interests and, second, that the categories of managerial staff and employees in positions of confidence are not so broadly defined that the organisations of other workers in the enterprise or branch of activity are weakened by depriving them of a substantial proportion of their present or potential membership.

Trade union pluralism and unity: the problem of trade union monopoly

132. While the right of workers to organise freely is subject in many countries to legislative and statutory provisions concerning the structure and composition of trade unions, the most important problems are linked to the system of trade union monopoly in countries where the legislation provides, directly or indirectly, that only one trade union may be established for a given category of workers, whether at the level of first-level organisations, or at every level of trade union organisation and for the trade union movement as a whole in the form of a hierarchical structure.

133. In some countries, the legislation only allows one first-level trade union organisation to be established for all the workers in an undertaking,[2] occupation or branch of activity.[3] In one country such a system has been established for a temporary period.[4] Moreover, in some countries, the provisions on the rights and functions of trade union committees, by assigning trade union functions only to a given trade union committee, appear to rule out the possibility of setting up another organisation representing workers of the same category. In other cases, the legislation establishes a monopoly either by expressly prohibiting the establishment of more than one organisation, or by

---

[1] See above, para. 86.

[2] For example, Bolivia (General Labour Act, s. 103); Colombia (Labour Code, ss. 357 and 364(i), and Decree No. 1373/1966, s. 11(1) and (2)); Guatemala (the Labour Code, s. 211(a), allows for the possibility of refusing to authorise the establishment of more than one trade union in an undertaking); Honduras (Labour Code, s. 472); Mexico (Federal Law for Workers in the Service of the State - for a given public service unit, ss. 68, 71-73); Nicaragua (Labour Code, s. 189); Panama (Labour Code, s. 346); Peru (Decree No. 021 of 1962).

[3] For example, United Republic of Cameroon (Order No. 24/MTLS/DEGRE, 1969, s. 4, para. 2); Mauritania (Labour Code, Book III, s. 1).

[4] Poland (the Trade Union Act, 1982 (s. 53) lays down a system of trade union monopoly in the undertaking for a transitional period to 31 December 1984).

fixing a percentage for membership which would make it impossible to
set up several organisations through requiring the participation of at
least 50 per cent of the workers concerned. The Committee considers
that the imposition of a system of trade union monopoly at the level of
the undertaking or of the occupation, in addition to being contrary to
Article 2 of the Convention, is also capable of facilitating acts of
interference by the employer or employers concerned.

134. While the first-level organisations, in a monopoly
situation, are sometimes free to form federations and confederations of
their own choosing, there is, however, reason for greater concern in
countries where the legislation imposes a single-trade-union system at
all levels of organisation. Pluralism is prohibited, directly, or
indirectly by law, not only at the local level, but also at the
regional and national levels. Only one first-level organisation and
one national trade union may be established for a given category of
workers, or only one federation for each category or region. These
organisations in turn may or must join a single national confederation
or trade union centre, which is sometimes specifically designated in
the law. Unitary or monopoly systems exist in an increasing number of
countries, although guided by different socio-economic and political
principles.[1] Sometimes legislation explicitly establishes a single
trade union system and sometimes such a system arises indirectly out of
a set of provisions. The result of such legal provisions is to make it
impossible to establish a second organisation representing workers'
interests. This is the case when legislation states expressly that
only one trade union may exist at all levels of trade union organisation and that trade unions are to be grouped together in a single confederation, when the establishment of a new trade union is subject to
the approval of the central management of the trade union which already
exists in the occupation concerned, when first-level organisations must
conform to the constitutions of the single existing central
organisation, when an organisation is obliged to affiliate to the
single central workers' union on penalty of remaining illegal, etc.

135. Moreover, in most countries where the legislation has
established, directly or indirectly, a single trade union system, the
trade union is, in addition, closely linked to the single party in
power,[2] which constitutes, for example, "the leading nucleus of all
social organisations" or "under whose leadership the trade union
organisation operates".

----

[1] For example, Bulgaria (Labour Code, s. 7); Burma (Act No. 76/1976
and Regulation No. 5/1976, Chapter 2); Burundi (Decision No. OC17/1980
establishing the UTB - Burundi Workers' Union); Congo (Labour Code,
Chapter V, Title VI); Cuba (Legislative Decree No. 3/77); Egypt (Trade
Union Act, ss. 7, 14 and 17; Ethiopia (Proclamation No. 222 of 1982,
on trade union organisations and No. 223 of 1982, on the consolidation
of peasant associations); Gabon (Labour Code, s. 174); German
Democratic Republic (Labour Code, s. 6); Iraq (Labour Law No. 151);
Kenya (New Industrial Relations Charter, 1980); Kuwait (Labour Law,
1964); Libyan Arab Jamahiriya (Act No. 107/75, ss. 1, 28 and 29); Mali
(Constitution of 1974 and Ordinances 77-24/CMLM and 77-7/CMLM); Nigeria
(Decree No. 22 of 1978); Poland (Law on Peasant Organisations, 1982,
s. 33); Syrian Arab Republic (Legislative Decree No. 84/1968); Tanzania
(JUWATA Act of 1979); Uganda (Trade Unions Decree No. 20 of 1976 and
Decree No. 29 of 1973); Yemen (Labour Code, ss. 138, 139 and 159);
Zambia (Industrial Relations Act, 1971).

[2] For example, Algeria, Angola, Czechoslovakia, Mongolia, Romania,
Seychelles, USSR.

136. All these various systems of trade union unity or monopoly imposed by law are at variance with the principle of free choice of workers' and employers' organisations contained in Article 2 of Convention No. 87. This principle was not intended as an expression of support either for the idea of trade union unity or for that of trade union pluralism. In many countries, there may be several organisations among which the workers or employers may wish to choose freely. In other countries however where no such diversity exists, workers and employers may wish to establish new organisations. Thus, although it was clearly never the purpose of the Convention to make trade union diversity an obligation, it does at least require this diversity to remain possible in all cases. There is a fundamental difference between a situation in which a trade union monopoly is instituted or maintained by law and the factual situation in which the workers or their trade unions join together voluntarily in a single organisation, without this being the result of legislative provisions adopted to this effect. Movements to consolidate or group together may occur among trade unions independently of the law or of pressure from the public authorities, on the decision of the trade unions themselves who may wish to group together for various reasons (for example, in order to strengthen their position at the bargaining table, to tackle the difficulties involved in structural and technological changes which affect the activity of trade unions, etc.).

137. However, the Committee would like to make it clear that, even in a case where a de facto monopoly exists as a consequence of all the workers having grouped together, legislation should not institutionalise this factual situation, for example, by designating the single central organisation by name, even if the existing trade union so requests. Even in a situation where, at some point in the history of a nation, all workers have preferred to unify the trade union movement, they should, however, be able to safeguard their freedom to set up, should they so wish in the future, unions outside the established trade union structure. In addition, the rights of workers who do not wish to join existing trade unions or the existing central organisation should also be protected.

138. While it is generally to the advantage of workers and employers to avoid proliferation of competing organisations, trade union unity directly or indirectly imposed by the law runs counter to the standards expressly laid down in the Convention.

Trade union monopoly and registration

139. A single-trade-union system may result, not from explicit provisions, but from provisions governing registration of trade unions. In some countries, the law gives the registrar some discretion in refusing registration of a trade union when there is already another registered union which, in his opinion, adequately represents the workers concerned, or if he considers that it is not in the interests of the workers concerned to register a new trade union.[1] Even if they do not expressly prohibit the establishment of more than one trade union for a given category of workers, provisions of this kind are not compatible with the provisions of the Convention because they may be used to bring about trade union unification and to establish or

----

[1] For example, Malaysia (Trade Unions Act, s. 12); Malawi (Trade Unions Act, s. 15); Singapore (Trade Unions Act, s. 14); Uganda (Trade Unions Act, 1976, s. 10).

maintain a situation of trade union monopoly. Legislative provisions concerning trade union registration which result in the rejection cf an application for registration if the authorities consider that a trade union adequately representing the interests of the workers concerned has already been registered, mean that in some cases employees may be denied the right to join the organisation of their choice, contrary to the principle of freedom of association.

140. In a system of optional registration, a similar situation results from legislative provisions which specifically designate one trade union for a given sector, precluding registration of any other trade union, or which stipulate that only one trade union may be set up in a given branch of industry.[1]

Trade union monopoly and representativity

141. In a large number of countries the law draws a distinction between the most representative trade union and other trade unions. This type of provision is not in itself contrary to the principle of freedom of association, provided that the distinction is limited to the recognition of certain rights - principally in regard to representation for the purposes of collective bargaining, consultation by governments, or designating representatives to international organisations - to the most representative trade union, determined according to objective and pre-established criteria. The possibility of such a distinction does not imply, however, that the existence of other trade unions which some of the workers concerned may wish to join or the activities of these trade unions may be prohibited. Minority organisations should be allowed to function and at least have the right to make representations on behalf of their members and to represent them in the case of individual grievances.

Trade union monopoly and trade union security

142. Taking account of the discussions held before the adoption of Convention No. 87 and the rejection by the Committee cn Freedom of Association of the International Labour Conference of an amendment to

----

[1] For example, Western Australia: the Public Service Arbitration Regulations, s. 11, and the Industrial Arbitration Act, s. 96, designate a specific trade union to represent the public service, ruling out the registration of any other trade union.

New Zealand: the Fishing Industry (Union Coverage) Act, 1979, authorises the establishment of only one new trade union in this industry, at the discretion of the Minister of Labour. With regard to this legislation, the Committee on Freedom of Association considered that "a situation in which an individual is denied any possibility of choice between different organisations by reason of the fact that the legislation permits the existence of only one organisation in the sphere in which he carries on his occupation, is incompatible with the principles of freedom of association" (204th Report, Case No. 956, para. 177).

grant workers the right not to join an organisation,[1] the Committee recognised that "Article 2 of the Convention leaves it to the practice and regulations of each State to decide whether it is appropriate to guarantee the right of workers not to join an occupational organisation, or on the other hand, to authorise and, where necessary, to regulate the use of union security clauses in practice".[2]

143. In many countries, the law guarantees directly or indirectly what is sometimes called "negative freedom of association", that is, the right not to join a trade union organisation, and forbids the exercise of any constraint which would oblige a person to adhere to or support a trade union.

144. In a number of other countries, the law allows "union security" clauses in collective agreements or arbitration awards. The legislation sometimes makes the utilisation of these clauses subject to certain conditions or prohibits specific types of union security arrangements. These clauses, which have the effect of making trade union membership or payment of union dues compulsory, may take different forms. Some specify that an employer can only recruit workers who are members of trade unions and who must remain union members in order to keep their job (the closed shop).[3] In other cases the employer may recruit the workers he chooses, but these must then join a trade union within a specified period (the union shop).[4] Without making trade union membership a condition of employment, other clauses make it compulsory for all workers, whether or not they are members of trade unions, to pay union dues or contributions (the agency shop).[5] Lastly, according to the principle of preferential treatment, the employer agrees to give preference to trade union members in respect of recruitment and other matters.[6] These clauses aim to strengthen the position of trade unions by ensuring that they become better

----

[1] ILO: Record of Proceedings, ILC, 30th Session, 1947, p. 571.

[2] RCE, Report III (Part IV), ILC, 43rd Session, 1959, p. 109, para. 36.

[3] For example, Japan, Mexico.

[4] For example, United Kingdom (the Trade Unions and Labour Relations Act, 1974, as amended in 1976, also allows "closed shop" clauses).

[5] For example, Switzerland (collective agreements may require payment of solidarity subscriptions by employees who do not belong to a trade union).

[6] For example, Australia, New Zealand.

In New Zealand (Industrial Relations Act, 1973) trade union affiliation is determined by the insertion in arbitration awards and collective agreements of an unqualified preference provision to the effect that any worker covered by the arbitration award or collective agreement must become a member of the union concerned within 14 days after his engagement.

The Committee has observed (ILO: RCE, General Survey, Report III (Part 4B), ILC, 58th Session, 1973, para. 77) that in New Zealand the right of registered unions to obtain the insertion of union security clauses (in the form of unqualified preference clauses) in binding arbitration awards of general application raises barriers against the creation and existence of unregistered unions. (See also para. 337, note 1.)

established among workers, by giving them greater weight vis-à-vis employers and by ensuring that all the employees who benefit from the work of the trade unions contribute to them fairly.[1]

145. The situation is altogether different when union security ceases to be based on clauses freely agreed upon between workers' unions and employers but is imposed by the law itself on workers. This is the case when the law makes it compulsory to join a union or when it designates a specific trade union as benefiting from the system,[2] or when the law establishes the system of compulsory trade union contributions in circumstances such that the same aim is achieved.[3] Such provisions are similar in their results to those establishing a trade union monopoly and are not compatible with the right of workers to establish and join organisations of their own choosing.

Coercion or favouritism by the government

146. Government action may influence the choice of workers regarding the organisation to which they intend to belong by placing one organisation at an advantage or at a disadvantage in relation to

---

[1] Some legislation allows exemption from union security clauses for persons who refuse to join a trade union because of conscientious or religious objections.

For example, Australia, Canada (British Columbia), New Zealand, United States (health care institution employers). In the United States, federal law protects, inter alia, the right of public servants to agree or to refuse to join or to support a trade union.

[2] For example, Canada. Some provincial legislative provisions entail compulsory membership or compulsory payment of trade union dues to organisations named in the law (Nova-Scotia, Ontario, Quebec). New Zealand (Waterfront Industry Act, 1976).

[3] See in this connection, the Committee on Freedom of Association's 181st Report, Case No. 857, paras. 100 and 101. In that case the negotiation fee payable by non-union members to the bargaining agent had been fixed at a very low level. The Committee on Freedom of Association considered that the fixing of the negotiation fee at such a low level could have the effect of discouraging those concerned from seeking membership of that union which is the bargaining agent, thus enabling them to remain non-unionists or members of another union.

Bahamas (Industrial Relations Act, ss. 43 A); Grenada (Act No. 1/82). These Acts establish a system of compulsory contributions to the trade union which has been certified as bargaining agent.

Congo (Decree No. 73-167 MJT); Gabon (Law No. 13/8C); Mali (Labour Code and Decree No. 1157/MT.CAB.1977); Nigeria (Decree No. 2/1978). In these countries the legal institution of the check-off system or trade union solidarity contributions in favour of the single existing organisation reinforces the trade union monopoly.

Tanzania (Law No. 1 of 1982). This law establishes a system of compulsory payments to the sole central union that exists in undertakings where more than 50 per cent of the workers are members of that central organisation.

the others. In this connection, the Committee on Freedom of Association has recalled that by placing one organisation at an advantage or at a disadvantage in relation to the others, a government may either directly or indirectly influence the choice of workers regarding the organisation to which they intend to belong, since they will undeniably want to belong to the union best able to serve them, even if their natural preference would have led them to join another organisation for occupational, religious, political or other reasons.[1]

*

*   *

147. Under Convention No. 87, workers and employers have the right to establish and join organisations of their own choosing. Put in these terms, the principle must be considered as one of the foundations of freedom of association. It entails in particular the right to determine the structure and composition of trade unions, to set up one or several organisations in any one enterprise, occupation or branch of activity, and to establish federations and confederations freely. Provisions fixing conditions which are too restrictive, particularly as regards the minimum number of members, and provisions which impose a single trade union system are incompatible with the guarantees laid down in the Convention. Any system of trade union monopoly imposed by law is at variance with the principle of free choice of organisations laid down in Article 2 of Convention No. 87. A tendency towards relative centralisation of the trade union movement may be observed in most countries. When these moves towards centralisation are made at the initiative of the trade unions themselves, and are an expression of their own spontaneous will, they are in conformity with Convention No. 87. On the other hand, trade union unity imposed by law at all levels runs counter to the Convention even if it is a result of a request made by the existing trade union organisation.

148. Although the Convention clearly does not aim to make trade union pluralism compulsory, pluralism must be possible in every case. Trade union unity imposed by law, whether directly or indirectly, runs counter to the principles of the Convention.

---

[1] In this connection, see ILO: Committee on Freedom of Association, 211th Report, Cases Nos. 1035 and 1050, para. 115.

CHAPTER VI

The right of organisations to draw up their constitutions and rules and to elect their representatives in full freedom

149. Article 3 of Convention No. 87 recognises four basic rights of workers' and employers' organisations: the right to draw up their constitutions and rules, the right to elect their representatives in full freedom, the right to organise their administration and their activities and the right to formulate their programe of action without interference from the public authorities.[1] When exercising such rights organisations are bound to respect the law, in accordance with Article 8 of the Convention, but the law of the land must not be such as to impair, or be so applied as to impair, the guarantees provided for in the Convention.

Constitutions and rules

150. In several countries, the legislation contains no special provisions relating to the contents of constitutions and rules of occupational organisations.[2] However, it is quite usual to find in trade union law certain prescriptions governing this matter, which may be fairly detailed on certain points, such as conditions of eligibility for trade union office, the election of officers, the management of funds, etc. In many countries, such provisions aim primarily to protect the rights of members, to provide for a sound administration and to prevent legal complications from arising at a later date as a result of constitutions being drawn up in insufficient detail; in other words, they do not restrict the right of organisations to draw up their constitutions and rules in freedom.

151. The question arises, however, as to whether it is always necessary for legislation to contain extremely detailed provisions on this subject. In practice, such provisions may impede the establishment and development of organisations. Legislation according to which union rules must comply with statutory requirements does not constitute an infringement of the principles of freedom of association

----

[1] Article 3(1). Workers' and employers' organisations shall have the right to draw up their constitutions and rules, to elect their representatives in full freedom, to organise their administration and activities and to formulate their programmes.

2. The public authorities shall refrain from any interference which would restrict this right or impede the lawful exercise thereof.

[2] For example, Belgium, Denmark, Federal Republic of Germany, France, Ireland, Italy, Ivory Coast, Luxembourg, Norway, Senegal.

provided that such requirements are purely formal and that approval of the rules is not within the discretionary power of the public authorities.[1]

152. There are, however, certain countries where the right of organisations to draw up their constitutions and rules appears to be considerably restricted. This may be the case, for example, where the law provides that a first-level trade union must conform to the constitution of the single existing federation,[2] or where the law makes the establishment of any new trade union subject to the approval of the central administration of the relevant occupational union which already exists,[3] or, again, where the sole central union has the exclusive right to elaborate the bye-laws of the unions and associations.[4] Such provisions are contrary to the Convention. There are extreme cases in two countries where the public authorities themselves drafted the constitutions of the central workers' organisations in these countries.[5]

153. In other cases, the law imposes a compulsory model constitution on trade unions.[6] The Committee considers that, with the exception of certain purely formal clauses, any obligation imposed on a trade union to base its constitution on a compulsory model runs counter to the principles ensuring freedom of association. The situation is different when the government merely makes specimen constitutions available to organisations in the process of creation without requiring them to accept the proposed model. The preparation of model constitutions and rules intended to serve as guidelines to trade unions, provided that there is no obligation to accept them, or any pressure exerted for this purpose, does not involve any interference with the right of trade union organisations to draw up their constitutions and rules in full freedom.

Election of representatives

154. While the laws of many countries contain no specific provisions concerning the right of organisations to elect their representatives, others, on the other hand, do contain specific provisions concerning conditions for eligibility and procedures for electing and removing trade union officers.

155. The Committee considers that the right of workers and employers to elect their representatives in full freedom is an

----

[1] Provisions making union rules subject to the discretionary approval of the authorities are not compatible with the Convention: for example, Argentina (Act No. 22105); Colombia (Labour Code, s. 369); Yemen (Labour Code, ss. 150 and 153).

[2] For example, Congo (Labour Code, Chapter V, Title VI); Romania (Labour Code, s. 964).

[3] For example, Bulgaria (Labour Code, s. 7).

[4] Ethiopia (Proclamations Nos. 222 and 223 of 1982).

[5] Kenya, Tanzania.

[6] Egypt, Law No. 35 of 1976 (as amended) on Trade Unions, ss. 31 and 61.

essential condition for their organisations to act effectively and
independently and to promote their members' interests efficiently. For
this right to be fully recognised, it is essential that the public
authorities refrain from any interference which would restrict the
exercise of this right, whether in determining the conditions of
eligibility of union officials or in the process of the elections
themselves.

Conditions of eligibility

156. Statutory provisions concerning eligibility requirements
for trade union office relate in particular to the following matters:
occupational requirements, nationality, political views or activities,
penal record and re-election.

157. Some provisions stipulate that candidates for trade union
office must belong to the occupation represented by the organisation or
be actually employed in this occupation, and sometimes that they must
have been employed in it for a certain period prior to the elections.[1]
Restrictions may also arise out of provisions requiring members of
trade unions to belong to the occupation concerned, coupled with
provisions requiring the officers of the organisation to be chosen from
among its members.[2]

158. In the Committee's opinion, provisions of this type may
prevent qualified persons, such as pensioners or full-time union
officers, from carrying out union duties; in addition, dismissal of a
union officer may prevent the person concerned from retaining his
office. Such provisions may also deprive unions of the benefit of the
experience of certain officers when they are unable to provide enough
qualified persons from their own ranks. When national legislation
provides that all trade union leaders shall belong to the occupation in
respect of which the organisation carries on its activities, the
guarantees laid down in the Convention may be impaired. In fact, in
such cases, the dismissal of a worker who is a trade union leader may,
by causing him to lose his status as a trade union officer, infringe
the freedom of activity of the organisation and its right to elect
representatives in freedom, and may even leave the way open for acts of
----

[1] For example, Argentina (Act No. 22105, s. 16 - four years'
service); Bangladesh (Act No. XXIX of 1980, s. 7a 1(a) and (b));
Central African Republic (Labour Code, s. 10 - five years' service);
Chile (Legislative Decree No. 2756/79, s. 21 - two years' service);
Colombia (Labour Code, ss. 388 and 422); Ecuador (Labour Code, s. 445);
Haiti (Labour Code, s. 276); Honduras (Labour Code, s. 510(c)); Lesotho
(Trade Union Law, 1964, s. 27); Libyan Arab Jamahiriya (Act No. 107/75,
s. 1); Malaysia (Trade Unions Act, s. 28); Malawi (Trade Unions Act, s.
28); Nicaragua (Trade Union Regulation, s. 24); Peru (Decree No. 001 of
1963); Syrian Arab Republic (Legislative Decree No. 84, ss. 44, 53, 61
and 66); Zambia (Industrial Relations Act, s. 18). In Malaysia (Trade
Unions Act, s. 30) and Zambia (Industrial Relations Act, s. 18), the
authorities may suspend this requirement or grant exemptions in the
case of certain unions or individuals. In Turkey, in order to be
elected as a trade union leader, a person must have been a worker for
at least two years (Constitution of 1982, art. 51).

[2] For example, Cyprus (Trade Union Law, ss. 20 and 57); Uruguay
(Trade Union Act and Regulation, ss. 5, 9, 39 and 47); Venezuela
(Labour Code, ss. 165 and 200).

interference by the employer. For the purpose of bringing legislation which restricts union office to persons actually employed in the occupation concerned into conformity with the principle of free election of representatives, it is necessary at least to make these provisions more flexible by admitting as candidates persons who have previously been employed in the occupation concerned and by exempting from the occupational requirement a reasonable proportion of the officers of an organisation.

159. In many cases, being a national of the country concerned is a condition of eligibility for trade union office.[1] Sometimes, such a condition is required only in the case of a certain proportion of the officers of a trade union[2] or is less strict, as for example where there is reciprocity between countries[3] or where the authorities have a discretionary power to grant exemptions from the statutory conditions of nationality.[4] Provisions on this matter which are too strict involve the risk of depriving certain categories of workers of the right to elect their representatives in full freedom. Problems of this type could arise, in particular, with the increasing migration of workers.

160. The Committee is of the opinion that such legislation should be flexible in order to permit organisations to choose their leaders without hindrance and also to permit foreign workers to hold trade union office, at least after a reasonable period of residence in the host country.[5] In this respect, the Migrant Workers Recommendation, 1975 (No. 151) states that equality of opportunity and treatment must apply to trade union rights and, in particular, eligibility for office in trade unions.[6]

161. Provisions concerning ineligibility for trade union office on political grounds are sometimes directed against activities of a

----

[1] For example, Algeria (Labour Code, Book III, ss. 4 and 2-5); Brazil (Consolidated Labour Laws, ss. 515 and 537 and Order 3437/1974, s. 12); Ecuador (Labour Code, s. 423); Honduras (Labour Code, ss. 510 and 541); Liberia (Labour Practices Act, s. 4102); Libyan Arab Jamahiriya (Act No. 107/1975, s. 11); Morocco (Dahir of 16 July 1957, s. 3); Mexico (Federal Labour Law, s. 372); Nicaragua (Labour Code, ss. 197 and 207); Niger (Labour Code, ss. 6 and 25); Rwanda (Labour Code, s. 8, for employees' organisations); Senegal (Labour Code, ss. 7 and 25); Upper Volta (Labour Code, ss. 6 and 24).

[2] Argentina (Trade Unions Act of 1979, s. 16).

[3] For example, Central African Republic (Labour Code, ss. 10 and 25); Ivory Coast (Labour Code, ss. 6 and 25); Mauritania (Labour Code, Book III, ss. 7 and 22).

[4] For example, Malaysia (Trade Unions Act, s. 30); Tunisia (Labour Code, ss. 251 and 252).

[5] This is the case, for example, in Chile (Legislative Decree No. 2756/79, s. 2); Congo (Labour Code, s. 187); Costa Rica (Labour Code, ss. 275 and 288); France (Labour Code, s. L.411-4); Gabon (Labour Code, ss. 6 and 24); Paraguay (Labour Code, ss. 290 and 305); Venezuela (Labour Code, ss. 173, 175 and 190).

[6] See, in this connection, para. 96 above.

subversive nature,[1] activities in a particular political party or movement[2] or the defence of ideological principles of a party whose registration has been cancelled or of an association whose activities are contrary to the national interest and whose registration has been cancelled or suspended.[3]

162. The Committee is of the opinion that legislation which deprives certain persons of the right to hold trade union office solely on the grounds of their political belief or affiliation is not compatible with the right of organisations to elect their representatives in full freedom.

163. Some legal systems contain provisions disqualifying from trade union office persons who have been convicted of almost any type of criminal offence,[4] or of certain specific crimes which are considered to make it inappropriate to place the guilty person in a position of trust such as trade union office.[5] In other cases, a penal record can result in the loss of civil or political rights, the possession of which is also a requirement, under the legislation of some countries, for eligibility for trade union office.

164. The Committee considers that conviction on account of offences the nature of which is not such as to call into question the integrity of the person concerned and is not such as to be prejudicial to the exercise of trade union functions should not constitute grounds for disqualification from trade union office and that legislation providing for disqualification on the basis of any offence is incompatible with the principles of freedom of association.

165. Legislation sometimes contains specific provisions imposing restrictions on the re-election of trade union officers. In some cases there is an absolute prohibition in this regard;[6] in others, the law

----

[1] For example, Australia (Australian Commonwealth Crimes Act, s. 30A).

[2] For example, Malaysia (the law disqualifies a candidate for trade union office if he is a leader or employee in a political party - Trade Unions Act, s. 28. Under s. 30 the Minister may, however, waive this restriction); United States (Labor-Management Reporting and Disclosure Act, 1959, s. 504, and Civil Service Reform Act, 1978, s. 7120).

[3] For example, Brazil (Order No. 3437/1974, s. 12).

[4] For example, Chile (Legislative Decree No. 2756/79, s. 21); Madagascar (Labour Code, s. 7); Uruguay (a person may be elected to trade union office only if he has not held positions of leadership in organisations which have been declared unlawful and has not been disqualified from election to trade union office, under a constitutional order - Regulation respecting Trade Unions No.513/981).

[5] For example, Argentina (Trade Unions Decree No. 640); Kenya (Trade Unions Ordinance, 1952, ss. 29 and 40); Tunisia (Labour Code, ss. 251 and 252), Uganda (Trade Unions Act, 1976, ss. 10, 22 and 23).

[6] For example, Guatemala (Labour Code, s. 222(a)); Mexico (in the case of public servants, Federal Law for Workers in the Service of the State, s. 31).

provides for exemptions or prohibits re-election only where a certain number of consecutive terms have been fulfilled.[1]

166. Whatever the provisions preventing officers from being re-elected, any legislation which prohibits or restricts re-election to trade union office is incompatible with the Convention. In addition, such a prohibition may entail serious consequences for the normal development of a trade union movement where the latter cannot count on an adequate number of persons capable of properly carrying out the duties of a trade union officer.

Election procedures

167. In the vast majority of countries, the law recognises, implicitly or explicitly, the principle of nomination of trade union officers by members.

168. In some cases the legislation does not contain any specific provisions on this subject[2] or only provides that the constitutions of trade union organisations must indicate the procedure for appointing their executive bodies[3] or include provisions concerning their executive bodies.[4]

169. In others the legislation contains certain rules intended to promote democratic principles within trade union organisations[5] or to ensure that the electoral procedure is conducted in a normal manner and with due respect for the rights of members in order to avoid any dispute arising as to the result of the election.[6] Provisions of this kind clearly do not involve any violation of the principles of freedom of association.

170. In addition to general principles, the legislation of some countries contains a great many specific rules relating to trade union elections,[7] sometimes providing for intervention by the administrative authorities in the supervision of the electoral procedure.

----

[1] For example, Nicaragua (Trade Union Regulations, s. 30 - prohibition of re-election for more than two consecutive terms); Uruguay (Trade Union Regulations, s. 19 - a certain interval must elapse before an officer may be re-elected).

[2] For example, Belgium, Byelorussian SSR, Czechoslovakia, Denmark, Federal Republic of Germany, Finland, Haiti, Hungary, Iceland, Ireland, Italy, Jordan, Luxembourg, Netherlands, Norway, Sweden, Trinidad and Tobago, Ukrainian SSR, United Kingdom, USSR, Yugoslavia.

[3] For example, Barbados, Botswana, Democratic Yemen, Ghana, Guyana, India, Jamaica, Malta, Nigeria, Poland, Sierra Leone, Sri Lanka.

[4] For example, Austria, Benin, Chad, Congo, France, Gabon, Guinea, Ivory Coast, Mali, Morocco, Niger, Togo, Tunisia.

[5] For example, Guatemala, Honduras, Mauritania.

[6] For example, Burundi, United Republic of Cameroon, Mexico, Pakistan, Paraguay, Rwanda, Somalia, Zaire.

[7] For example, Argentina, Bangladesh Brazil, Chile, Colombia, El Salvador, Guatemala, Honduras, Japan, Malaysia, Paraguay, Singapore, United States.

171. Lastly, in some countries,[1] the legislation in force prescribes approval or ratification of the results by the Minister of Labour and even, in a few rare cases, nomination of at least part of the executive committee by the public authorities.[2]

172. The Committee considers that legislation which regulates in detail the internal election procedures of trade unions is incompatible with the rights of trade unions recognised by Convention No. 87. There is reason to believe that detailed regulation of trade union elections, by legislation which prescribes specific rules on the subject, limits the right of organisations to elect their representatives in full freedom and may constitute a kind of a priori supervision of the electoral procedure, making it easier for the public authorities to intervene in the voting process.

173. The Committee considers that legislative provisions prescribing the intervention of certain administrative authorities in the election procedure (for example, the obligatory presence of labour inspectors or of representatives of the labour administration during voting or the participation of these officials in the counting of votes) create a risk of interference which is not compatible with Convention No. 87. Even if the provisions in question are aimed at preventing disputes or guaranteeing respect for constitutions and the law, the intervention of the administrative authorities is liable to appear arbitrary, and it is desirable that supervision, if it is necessary, should be exercised by the competent judicial authority so as to guarantee an impartial procedure.

174. As regards election results, the Committee considers that there is interference on the part of the administrative authorities, which is incompatible with Convention No. 87, where the results must be approved by the Ministry of Labour or where the election is valid only after being approved by the administrative authorities. Nomination of trade union officers by the public authorities also constitutes interference which is clearly incompatible with the Convention.

Dismissal of trade union officers

175. Dismissal of trade union officers may be the outcome of an internal decision of the trade union, usually after a vote by members, or of measures taken by the public authorities, whether they be of an administrative or a judicial nature.

176. Problems of conformity with the Convention arise in particular when the administrative authorities are empowered to suspend or dismiss union officers,[3] or when the council of the single central trade union federation has the right to dissolve the executive board of

----

[1] For example, Argentina, Australia, Colombia, Liberia, Malaysia, New Zealand, Panama, Philippines, Singapore, Sudan.

[2] For example, Kenya (Presidential Decree of 1965); Tanzania (Ordinance on trade unions and JUWATA Act).

[3] For example, Brazil (Consolidated Labour Laws, ss. 553 and 557); Colombia (Labour Code, s. 380); Kenya (Presidential Decision, 1965).

any trade union organisation.[1] The same is true where dismissals are ordered under the terms of an Act or special decree promulgated for this purpose.[2]

177. In the opinion of the Committee, the suspension or removal of trade union officers, in cases where violations of the legislation or of union rules have been proved in the course of judicial proceedings, as well as the appointment of temporary administrators, should be effected only through the courts. In addition, the law should fix criteria which are specific enough to enable the judicial authority to ascertain whether a trade union officer has committed such acts as would justify his suspension or dismissal. Legal provisions which are too general or provisions which do not respect the principles laid down in the Convention do not constitute an adequate guarantee in this respect. When administrative measures exist for the dismissal, disqualification or suspension of trade union officers, taken in application of legal provisions, they should not become enforceable until the period allowed for the persons concerned to lodge an appeal to wholly independent judicial authorities has expired. Lastly, legislative measures taken by the public authorities governing the dismissal of trade union officers should only be aimed at protecting the rights of members, preventing abuses of authority on the part of leaders of the organisation and, if necessary, preventing complex legal problems from arising in the event of an internal dispute.

* * *

178. Intervention by the public authorities in the drawing up of trade union rules and in election and dismissal procedures creates a serious risk of improper interference in the internal affairs of organisations.

179. The nature of the authorities called upon to intervene is therefore of prime importance as regards respect for the principles of freedom of association. The Committee considers that these principles do not preclude outside control of the internal activities of an organisation if it is considered or alleged that the law or rules have been infringed. However, where intervention relates to the election or dismissal of trade union officers or the placing of organisations under control, the measures taken by the administrative authorities are liable to be arbitrary. For this reason, and in order to guarantee an impartial and objective procedure, such control, if it is necessary, must be exercised by wholly independent judicial authorities.

----

[1] For example, Syrian Arab Republic (Legislative Decree No. 84, 1964, s. 49).

[2] Bolivia (Act No. 11947 of 1974); Canada (Quebec: Act No. 29 of 1975. This Act was adopted following the conclusions of a national commission of inquiry).

CHAPTER VII

Right of workers' and employers' organisations to organise their administration and activities and to formulate their programmes

180. Article 3 of Convention No. 87 provides that workers' and employers' organisations have the right "to organise their administration and activities and to formulate their programmes" and that "the public authorities shall refrain from any interference which would restrict this right or impede the lawful exercise thereof".

181. As with the other rights guaranteed by Article 3, the principle of non-interference by the public authorities, recognised in paragraph 2 of this Article, is essential to protect the free exercise by the organisations of the right to organise their administration and activities and to formulate their programmes.

Administration

182. As indicated in Chapter VI above, trade union legislation in many countries contains provisions relating to the contents of the constitutions and rules of organisations, particularly as regards the management of funds. The purpose of these provisions is often to protect the rights of the members and to provide for a sound administration and, as such, they are not incompatible with the Convention.

183. Generally speaking, trade unions are required to include in their rules all relevant provisions concerning the source of the organisation's funds (admission fees, if any, regular contributions, special contributions and dues, fines, if any), the use of its funds, its internal financial administration and, sometimes, the distribution of assets in the event that the organisation is dissolved, wound up or merged. These provisions are mainly intended to ensure as far as possible the honest and efficient management of union funds and other assets.

184. Many countries have specific legislative provisions on the subject, generally designed to prevent abuses and to protect the members against bad administration of their funds.

185. Sometimes, however, the legislation confers on the public authorities extensive powers whereby they can exercise permanent control over the administration of funds. This is the case in countries where the law establishes the minimum contribution of members,[1] specifies the proportion of union funds that has to be paid

----

[1] For example, Ecuador (Labour Code, s. 443); India (Trade Unions Act, s. 6).

to the federations,[1] or requires that the budget, expenditure or investment of a trade union must be approved by the public authorities.[2] In some countries organisations are prohibited by law from receiving funds from abroad without the prior authorisation of the ministry of labour.[3]

186.   The legislation of many countries stipulates that periodic financial reports (usually annual) must be submitted to the competent authorities, which are often empowered to request additional information on any point that is not clear. The degree of supervision that may be exercised by the authorities sometimes exceeds a formal requirement that unions must furnish financial returns at regular intervals. In such cases the ministry of labour[4] or the registrar[5] may apparently request information or inspect books of account practically at any time. There are also countries whose legislation contains provisions relating to the investigation by the authorities of union finances or of internal union matters in general. In these cases the authorities are empowered to intervene when they presume that certain irregularities have occurred or when they have received complaints from union members.

187.   The Committee considers that, although the application of legislative provisions and union rules concerning an organisation's administration must by and large be left to the members of the trade union, the principles set out in the Convention do not exclude external control of the internal acts of an organisation where they are alleged or where there are major reasons for believing them to be against the law (which should not of course infringe the principles of freedom of association) or the union's constitution.

188.   Supervision of union finances should not normally go beyond a requirement for the organisation to submit periodic financial returns. If, on the other hand, the administrative authority has
----

[1] For example, Iraq (Labour Code).

[2] For example, Syrian Arab Republic.

[3] Philippines (Labour Code, s. 271); Zambia (Industrial Relations Act and information supplied by the Government). See also para. 250 below.

[4] For example, Argentina (Act No. 22105/1979 on occupational associations); Bolivia (General Labour Act, s. 101); Colombia (Labour Code, s. 486); Costa Rica (Labour Code, ss. 275 and 279); Dominican Republic (Resolution No. 13/1974); Haiti (Labour Code, s. 278); Kuwait (Labour Act, s. 76); Libyan Arab Jamahiriya (Act No. 107/1975, ss. 18-22); Nicaragua (Labour Code, s. 36); Panama (Labour Code, s. 376(4)); Philippines (Labour Code, s. 275); Syrian Arab Republic (Decree No. 84, ss. 32, 34 and 35, and Legislative Decree No. 250, s. 6).

[5] For example, Bangladesh (Industrial Relations Ordinance, s. 10); Ghana (Trade Unions Ordinance, s. 26); India (Trade Unions Act, s. 26); Kenya (Trade Unions Ordinance, s. 50); Nigeria (Decree No. 31/73, ss. 42-43); Pakistan (Industrial Relations Ordinance, s. 8); Trinidad and Tobago (Trade Unions Ordinance, s. 16).

In Malaysia (Trade Unions Act, s. 57) and Singapore (Trade Unions Act, s. 53), the Registrar is empowered to verify the administration of union funds at any "reasonable" moment.

discretionary power to examine the books and other documents of an organisation, conduct an investigation and demand information at any given time, there is a grave danger of interference which may be of such a nature as to restrict the guarantees provided for in Convention No. 87. Investigatory measures should be restricted to exceptional cases, when they are justified by special circumstances such as presumed irregularities that are apparent from annual financial statements or complaints reported by members of the trade union. Furthermore, in order to guarantee the impartiality and objectivity of the procedure, these controls should be conducted subject to review by the competent judicial authority. Legislation which empowers the administrative authorities to investigate the internal affairs of a union at their entire discretion does not conform to the principles of the Convention.[1]

Inviolability of union premises, correspondence and communications

189. Freedom to administer a trade union implies that it should be able to dispose of its assets unhindered and that the public authorities should refrain from interfering without due cause with the organisation's premises and correspondence.

190. Although most legal systems provide for the protection of private premises, and therefore of union premises and correspondence, they often make exceptions in emergency situations or in the interests of public order. While recognising that, as for any other associations or individuals, a trade union cannot claim immunity against the searching of its premises, the Committee considers that it should only be possible for such action to be taken when a warrant has been issued for the purpose by the regular judicial authority, when the authority is satisfied that there is good reason to presume that such a search will produce evidence for criminal proceedings under the ordinary law and provided the search is restricted to the purpose for which the warrant was issued.

Activities and programmes

191. Workers' and employers' organisations should have the right to organise their activities and formulate their programmes in complete freedom. Although this would appear to be the case in a substantial number of countries, some impose certain legal restrictions on the

----

[1] In the case of Uruguay, the Committee noted with satisfaction in 1982 that Act No. 15137/1981 and Regulation No. 513/981 represented a considerable improvement over the original draft Bill; in particular, the limitation on the duration of trade union assemblies and the extensive powers accorded to the public authorities to request reports on trade union activities had been removed.

With regard to Barbados, the Committee noted with satisfaction in 1975 an amendment to section 35 of the Trade Unions Act enabling trade unions to appeal to the Supreme Court against decisions of the Registrar of Trade Unions concerning violations of the regulations on the use of union funds.

guarantees provided for under the Convention, in particular on political activities and the right to strike.[1]

Political activities

192. In certain countries the law restricts the political activities of trade unions, for example by prohibiting them from making financial contributions to a political party or to persons seeking a political appointment.[2]

193. Elsewhere, there is a total ban on political activities. In many cases, for instance, the law prohibits the organisations purely and simply from engaging in party politics or any political activity whatsoever.[3]

194. By contrast, legislative or other provisions in certain countries establish close links between the trade unions and the sole political party in power.[4]

195. It is increasingly apparent, as was mentioned during the preparatory work on Convention No. 87,[5] that a trade union's activities cannot be restricted solely to occupational questions, since the choice of a general policy - in economic affairs for example - is bound to have consequences on the situation of workers (remuneration, holidays, working conditions, the running of enterprises, etc.). Developments in the trade union movement show that the promotion of working conditions through collective bargaining, though still a major feature of trade union action, increasingly involves participation by organisations in economic and social policy making bodies. This in turn means that trade unions must be able to devote attention to matters of general interest - i.e. "political" in the broadest sense of the word - and that, for example, they must be able to express their views publicly on a government's economic and social policy, since the fundamental objective of the trade union movement is to ensure the development of the social and economic well-being of all workers.
----

[1] As for restrictions on collective bargaining, see below, Chapter XII.

[2] For example, Liberia (Labour Practices Law, s. 411O).

[3] For example, Argentina (Act No. 22105/1979, s. 8); Brazil (Consolidated Labour Laws, s. 521); Chad (Labour Code, s. 36); Colombia (Labour Code, s. 378a, Decree No. 2655/1954 and Resolution No. 4/1952); Costa Rica (Labour Code, s. 280); El Salvador (Labour Code, s. 229(a)); Ecuador (Labour Code, s. 443); Kuwait (Labour Act, s. 73); Nicaragua (Labour Code, s. 204); Paraguay (Labour Code, s. 302); Peru (Decree No. 009/1961); Somalia (Labour Code, s. 28); Turkey (1982 Constitution, Art. 52).

In the case of _Madagascar_, the Committee noted with _satisfaction_ in 1976 that the new Labour Code eliminated a sentence in the previous Code forbidding trade unions to engage in any political activity.

[4] See para. 135 above.

[5] During the preparatory work on Convention No. 87, the Workers' members and several Government members opposed any amendment of the text proposed by the Office that might restrict trade union activities solely to occupational matters. See ILO, _Record of Proceedings_, ILC, 30th Session, 1947, p. 570.

196. However, as the International Labour Conference indicated in its 1952 resolution concerning the independence of the trade union movement, when trade unions in accordance with the law and practice of their respective countries and at the decision of their members decide to establish relations with a political party or to undertake constitutional political action as a means towards the advancement of their economic and social objectives, such political relations or actions should not be of such a nature as to compromise the continuance of the trade union movement or its social and economic functions, irrespective of political changes in the country.

197. Moreover, when governments endeavour to enlist the collaboration of the trade unions in the implementation of their economic and social policy, they should appreciate that the value of such collaboration depends largely on the freedom and independence of the trade union movement, as an essential factor in social progress, and should not seek to transform it into a political instrument for the attainment of their own political objectives. Finally, they should not attempt to interfere in the normal activities of a union under the pretext of its freely established relationship with a political party.

198. The Committee therefore considers that legislative provisions prohibiting all political activities or, on the contrary, establishing a close link between the unions and a political party are incompatible with the principles of the Convention.

Protest action and the right to strike

199. Workers' organisations have a number of means at their disposal to promote and defend their economic and social interests. Some of these are simple protest actions, for example protest meetings or petitions, which do not cause any direct damage to the employer. Others, however, are aimed at exerting pressure by causing prejudice to the employer, e.g. slowing down of work (go-slow), the strict application of the rules (work-to-rule), or recourse to strike action.

200. The Committee considers that the right to strike is one of the essential means available to workers and their organisations for the promotion and protection of their economic and social interests. These interests not only have to do with obtaining better working conditions and pursuing collective demands of an occupational nature, but also with seeking solutions to economic and social policy questions and to labour problems of any kind which are of direct concern to the workers.[1]

201. In international law, the right to strike is explicitly recognised in Article 8 of the International Covenant on Economic, Social and Cultural Rights. At the regional level, the European Social Charter was the first international text to recognise explicitly the right to strike in the case of a conflict of interests, subject to any commitments under collective agreements in force.

202. The study of national legislation shows that the extent to which the right to strike is recognised differs from country to country: while tacitly or explicitly accepted in some countries, in many others it is limited by restrictions of varying scope and severity.

----

[1] See, for example, ILO: Committee on Freedom of Association, 214th Report, Case No. 1081, para. 261.

203. As regards the majority of the socialist countries, their legislation contains no provision relating to the legality or illegality of a strike. In view of the nature of the particular economic and political systems of these countries, the governments consider that trade unions have no need to resort to direct action in order to defend their interests.

General prohibition of strikes

204. A general prohibition of strikes and the suspension of the right to strike, such as occurs in certain countries, may arise from specific provisions in the law.[1] The prohibition of strikes may also result, for all practical purposes, from the cumulative effect of the provisions relating to the established dispute settlement machinery, according to which labour disputes are channeled through compulsory conciliation and arbitration procedures leading to a final award or decision which is binding on the parties concerned; a similar situation may arise in cases where, in the absence of an agreement between the parties, disputes can be settled by compulsory arbitration or decision at the discretion of the public authorities.[2] Under these systems, it is possible to prohibit or put a rapid stop to almost any strike.

205. A general ban on strikes seriously limits the means at the disposal of trade unions to further and defend the interests of their members (Article 10 of the Convention) and their right to organise their activities (Article 3) and is, therefore, not compatible with the principles of freedom of association.

206. A general prohibition of strikes or a temporary suspension of the right to strike sometimes results from provisions adopted under

---

[1] For example, Argentina (Act No. 21261/1976 prorogued by Act No. 21400/1976); Bangladesh (Ordinance No. XXVI/1982, s. 8); Chad (Ordinance No. 30/1975); Colombia (for federations and confederations, Labour Code, s. 417); Liberia (Decree No. 12/1980); Nicaragua (Decrees Nos. 911/1981 and 955/1982); Pakistan (Proclamation of 16 October 1979); Syrian Arab Republic (Agricultural Labour Code, s. 160); Thailand (Decree No. 3/1976, read in conjunction with ss. 133 and 141 of the Industrial Relations Act).

[2] For example, Algeria (Act No. 82-05,, ss. 40-42); Bolivia (General Labour Act, s. 113(c)); Brazil (Consolidated Labour Laws, s. 872); Colombia (Act No. 48/1968, s. 3); Cyprus (Rule 79B); Dominican Republic (Labour Code, ss. 374, 377, 633 and 655); Ecuador (Constitution, Article 31K and Labour Code, s. 466); Ethiopia (Labour Proclamation of 1975, ss. 99 and 106); Gabon (Labour Code, s. 239 et seq.); Ghana (Industrial Relations Act, 1965, ss. 18 and 21); India (Industrial Disputes Act, 1947, s. 10); Jamaica (Labour Relations and Industrial Disputes Act, 1975, as amended, s. 15); Kenya (Trade Disputes Act, 1965, ss. 21 and 22); Lesotho (Laws Nos. 34 of 1975 and 21 of 1982); Malaysia (Industrial Relations Act, s. 26); Malta (Industrial Relations Act, s. 27); Mauritius (Industrial Relations Act, ss. 82-83); Mauritania (Labour Code, Book IV, ss. 40 and 48); Nigeria (Industrial Disputes Decree No. 7/1976); Paraguay (Labour Procedure Code); Singapore (Industrial Relations Act, s. 31); Sri Lanka (Industrial Disputes Act, ss. 40 and 43); Sudan (Industrial Relations Act, 1976, ss. 17-31); Tanzania (Permanent Labour Tribunal Act, 1967, s. 22); Tunisia (Labour Code, ss. 384 to 387); Zambia (Industrial Relations Act, 1971).

emergency powers or may be attributed by governments to the existence
of a crisis. The Committee considers that, inasmuch as the prohibition
or general suspension of strikes constitutes a major restriction cf one
of the essential means available to workers and their organisations for
furthering and defending their interests, such measures cannct be
justified except in a situation of acute national crisis, and then only
for a limited period.

Specific restrictions on the right to strike

207. In some countries the legislation, while admitting the
principle of the right to strike, introduces a number cf more or less
important restrictions on such action: these restrictions concern
certain categories of workers; or they are imposed in the light of the
objectives of the strike or the methods employed; or they are derived
from provisions imposing time limits which must elapse before workers
can resort to strike action.[1]

Restrictions relating to public servants and workers in essential services

208. National legislations differ radically on the subject of
the legality or otherwise of work stoppages decided by public servants.
A comparison of current legislation in a number of countries shows that
a variety of possibilities are provided for, along with several
possible solutions.

209. At one extreme there are countries whose legislaticn
specifically recognises the right to strike of public servants[2] and
where, if a dispute can be settled neither by existing machinery nor
through consultation or negotiation, they can lawfully engage in strike
action. The laws and regulaticns in force may, however, restrict the
exercise of this right by people in certain positions.[3]

210. Some countries make no distinction between strikes in the
public sector and strikes in other sectors of the economy: public
servants must simply observe the normal procedure laid down in the
general legislation of the country.[4]

211. In another group of countries, there are no laws or
regulations concerning the legality or otherwise of strikes by public
----

[1] With regard to Panama, the Committee noted with satisfaction in
1982 that Act No. 8/1981 had removed the limitation imposed on the
exercise of the right to strike which made such exercise subject to the
condition that the demands for better working conditions made by
workers should not, in the opinion of the administrative authcrity,
affect the profitability of the undertaking.

[2] For example, Benin, Canada, Comoros, Finland, France, Greece,
Ivory Coast, Luxembourg, Mexico, Niger, Norway, Portugal, Senegal,
Sweden, Togo, Zaire.

[3] See para. 212 below.

[4] For example Italy and Sweden.

servants. Since the silence of the legislation on the matter is open to different interpretations, various legal solutions have been adopted by the countries concerned in such cases. On the one hand, the legality of a strike may be tacitly recognised or implied by the government's attitude towards the recognition or registration of trade unions.[1] (If a trade union's constitution, rules or other documents that have to be submitted to a competent authority provide for strike action and the authority does not raise any objection, it can be assumed that work stoppages are legal.) On the other hand, the issue may remain a matter of controversy.[2] Finally, the absence of any general or specific provisions relating to strikes in the public service may be interpreted as their tacit prohibition.[3] In a number of countries, the legislation explicitly denies the right of public servants to strike.[4]

212. Even the fact that the right to strike in the public service is explicitly or tacitly recognised does not mean that all public servants enjoy unlimited freedom in this respect. On the contrary, various limitations and restrictions have been introduced by law and in practice in a considerable number of countries that authorise strikes in the public service. These restrictions appear to be based on a variety of criteria, such as the level of responsibility of the officials concerned, their place in the administration hierarchy, the nature of the services they perform and the conditions in which a strike is called and conducted.[5]

213. Numerous countries also have provisions prohibiting or limiting strikes in essential services. However, the concept of essential services varies from one national legislation to another. In some cases, a long list of such services is given in the law itself;[6]

----

[1] For example, Israel, Madagascar, United Kingdom.

[2] For example, Austria, Belgium, Denmark, Netherlands.

[3] For example, Federal Republic of Germany.

[4] For example, Bolivia, Brazil, Burundi, Chile, Colombia, Costa Rica, Ecuador, Guatemala, Honduras, Kuwait, Lebanon, Morocco, Nicaragua, Philippines, Rwanda, Switzerland, Syrian Arab Republic, Thailand, Trinidad and Tobago, United States, Uruguay, Zimbabwe.

[5] For example, Canada, Finland, Japan, Luxembourg, Madagascar, Mexico, Norway.

[6] For example, Brazil (Legislative Decree No. 1642/1978); United Republic of Cameroon (Labour Code, s. 165, paragraph 3, and Decree No. 74/969, s. 2); Canada (the legislation of the Province of Alberta); Colombia (Labour Code, s. 430 and Decrees Nos. 414/1952, 1593/1959, 1167/1963 and 57 and 534/1967); Costa Rica (Labour Code, s. 369; however, subsection (b) of s. 369 (concerning transport and port work) has been declared unconstitutional); Dominican Republic (Labour Code, ss. 370 and 371); Guyana (Law on Public Utilities, Cap. 54:01); India (Essential Services Maintenance Act, No. 40, 1981); Jamaica (Labour Relations and Industrial Disputes Act, 1975, as amended, ss. 15 and 28); Kenya (Trade Disputes Act, 1965); Lesotho (Act No. 34/1975, amended in 1982); Malawi (Trade Disputes (Arbitration and Settlement) Ordinance); Pakistan (Industrial Relations Ordinance, ss. 31-33); Poland (Trade Unions Act, 1982, s. 40(1) and (2)); Sri Lanka (Essential Services Act, 1979); Swaziland (Industrial Relations Act, 1980, s. 65 and Note No. 54/1982); United States (Labor-Management Relations Act,

(Footnote continued on next page)

sometimes, the definition of such services covers all activities which the government may consider appropriate or all strikes that may be contrary to public order, the general interest or economic development.[1]

214. In the opinion of the Committee, the principle whereby the right to strike may be limited or prohibited in the public service or in essential services, whether public, semi-public or private, would become meaningless if the legislation defined the public service or essential services too broadly. As the Committee has already mentioned in previous general surveys,[2] the prohibition should be confined to public servants acting in their capacity as agents of the public authority or to services whose interruption would endanger the life, personal safety or health of the whole or part of the population.[3] Moreover, if strikes are restricted or prohibited in the public service or in essential services, appropriate guarantees must be afforded to protect workers who are thus denied one of the essential means of defending their occupational interests. Restrictions should be offset by adequate impartial and speedy conciliation and arbitration procedures, in which the parties concerned can take part at every stage and in which the awards should in all cases be binding on both parties. Such awards, once rendered, should be rapidly and fully implemented.

(Footnote continued from previous page)

1947, ss. 206-210); Venezuela (Labour Act (Regulations), s. 393); Zambia (Industrial Relations Act, s. 3).

In New Zealand, the Industrial Relations Act, 1973, lays down certain procedures to be followed before calling a strike in essential industries and export slaughterhouses (sections 125 and 125A). The Trade Act, 1975, authorises the Court of Arbitration to order a resumption of work on the grounds that the economy of the country is or may be seriously affected by a strike. A request to this effect may be addressed to the Court by a Minister or by a person directly affected by the strike (section 119C). Finally, an amendment to the Industrial Relations Act adopted in 1981 confers special powers on the Minister of Labour in the event of a strike or threat of strike in essential industries and export slaughterhouses affecting the public interest (section 125B-E).

[1] For example, Cyprus (Supply and Services (Transitional Powers) (Continuation) Law, Cap. 175A); Philippines (Labour Code, s. 264); Trinidad and Tobago (Industrial Relations Act, s. 65); Tunisia (Labour Code, s. 389).

[2] See RCE, Report III (Part IV), ILC, 43rd Session, 1959, para. 68, and General Surveys of 1973, para. 109, on freedom of association and collective bargaining and of 1978 on forced labour, para. 123. See also, ILO: Committee on Freedom of Association, 218th Report, Case No. 1131, para. 779.

[3] The Committee on Freedom of Association has, for example, considered that the hospital sector and air traffic control are essential services; but it has considered that banking, agricultural activities, ports, the metal, petrol, tobacco, and printing industries, teaching and radio and television, for example, are not essential services in the strict sense of the term.

Requisitioning, minimum service

215. Under the legislation of some countries, workers on strike can be requisitioned.[1] The requisitioning of workers could be abused as a means of settling labour disputes, and such action is therefore to be avoided except where, in particularly serious circumstances, essential services have to be maintained. Requisitioning may be justified by the need to ensure the operation of essential services in the strict sense of the term. In other sectors of the economy, on the other hand, the Committee considers that, if a total and prolonged stoppage of work in a major industrial sector is liable to endanger the life, safety or health of the population and cause an acute national emergency, the maintenance of a minimum service - concerning a specified category of workers - would seem to be justified. For such a measure to be acceptable, the minimum service should be restricted to operations that are strictly necessary to avoid endangering the life, personal safety or health of the whole or part of the population; at the same time, the workers' organisations should, if they wish, be able to participate in defining the minimum service along with the employers and public authorities.[2] Such a system could also be used in the case of essential services in order to avoid a total ban on strikes in these services.

Restrictions relating to the objectives of a strike

216. In many countries political strikes are explicitly or tacitly recognised as unlawful. Elsewhere, restrictions on strikes can be applied in such a way that any strike may be considered as threatening the security of the State. The Committee considers that trade union organisations ought to have the possibility of recourse to protest strikes, in particular where aimed at criticising a government's economic and social policies. However, strikes that are purely political in character do not fall within the scope of the principles of freedom of association.[3]

217. As for sympathy strikes, where workers come out in support of another strike, they are recognised as lawful in certain countries.[4] It would appear that more frequent recourse is being had to this form

---

[1] For example, Cyprus (Supply and Services (Transitional Powers) (Continuation) Law, Cap. 175A); Portugal (Legislative Decree No. 637/74); Tunisia (Labour Code, s. 389); Upper Volta (Ordinance No. 82.003/1982).

[2] See, for example, ILO: Committee on Freedom of Association, 204th Report, Case No. 952, para. 162; 221st Report, Case No. 1097, para. 84. In Greece, for essential services, only a minimum service must be ensured in the case of a strike. The unions participate in defining the number and composition of the teams required for the essential service (Law No. 1264, 1982, s. 21).

[3] See, for example, ILO: Committee on Freedom of Association, 139th Report, Cases Nos. 737-744, para. 124.

[4] For example, France, Federal Republic of Germany, India, Italy, Spain (in its ruling of 8 April 1981 the Constitutional Tribunal considered that the provision declaring sympathy strikes unlawful was unconstitutional in that it tended to limit the exercise of the right to strike to those "directly" concerned), Sweden, United Kingdom.

of action because of the structure or the concentration of industries or the distribution of work centres in different regions of the world. The Committee considers that a general prohibition of sympathy strikes could lead to abuse and that workers should be able to take such action provided the initial strike they are supporting is itself lawful.

Restrictions relating to the methods used

218. Where the right to strike is guaranteed by a country's legislation, the first question that arises is whether the action taken by the workers constitutes a strike as defined by the law. Normally speaking, any work stoppage can be described as a strike, however short or limited it may be. The problem would seem to be more complicated, however, where there is no stoppage but merely a slowing down of work (go-slow) or the strict application of the rules (work to rule). Staggered, sit-down and lightning strikes, repeated walk-outs and picketing also pose a problem. The Committee shares the opinion of the Committee on Freedom of Association that, as far as the methods of exercising the right to strike are concerned, restrictions on working to rule, the occupation of an enterprise or working premises, sit-down strikes and picketing can only be justified if the action ceases to be peaceful.

Provisions imposing a waiting period on strikes

219. In a large number of countries the law requires notice to be given of an intention to strike, allows for a cooling-off period or stipulates that the majority of the workers concerned or the general assembly of the union must first signify their approval of a strike order.[1] Such procedures should not be so cumbersome as to render the lawful strike impossible in practice.

220. The legislation of many countries requires workers to notify the administrative authorities of an intention to strike and to resort to conciliation and arbitration procedures before a strike is allowed to commence.[2]

221. Finally, there is the special situation in some countries where trade unions, having voluntarily decided to register with the authorities (which in turn entitles them to use the official machinery for the settlement of labour disputes by means of conciliation and arbitration proceedings with binding awards), are not allowed to strike

----

[1] For example, Burundi, Denmark, Honduras, Philippines, Poland, Switzerland, United Kingdom/Hong Kong, United States.

[2] In this regard, in countries where conciliation and arbitration are voluntary, due account should be taken of the Voluntary Conciliation and Arbitration Recommendation, 1951 (No. 92), whose Paragraph 7 states that "no provision of this Recommendation may be interpreted as limiting in any way whatsoever the right to strike". As to compulsory conciliation and arbitration procedures, which can in practice be tantamount to a ban on strikes, the Committee draws attention to the comments in paragraph 204 above.

if a strike ban has been included in an award or where they are bound by the terms of an award.[1]

Sanctions against strikes

222. Most legislation that restricts the right to strike contains clauses providing for sanctions against workers who infringe these provisions. In some countries, striking illegally is a penal offence punishable by a fine or term of imprisonment.[2] Elsewhere, engaging in an unlawful strike may be considered an unfair practice and incur the corresponding civil action and disciplinary sanctions.

223. As regards strikes the Committee considers that penal sanctions should only be imposed where there are violations of strike prohibitions which are in conformity with the principles of freedom of association. In addition, in these cases the sanctions should be proportionate to the offences committed, and penalties of imprisonment should not be imposed in the case of peaceful strikes. The Committee considers that the application of disproportionate penal sanctions does not favour the development of harmonious industrial relations.

*
* *

224. Interference by the administrative authorities in trade union activities may raise difficulties in the application of Article 3 of Convention No. 87, particularly where an organisation's financial administration is concerned. The principles embodied in the Convention do not exclude the possibility of external control over the internal activities of an organisation if it is believed or alleged that the law or a union's rules are being infringed. In order to guarantee an impartial and objective procedure, however, such control should be subject to review by independent judicial authorities. Similarly, the inviolability of the premises and correspondence of trade union organisations should be secured by judicial guarantees.

----

[1] For example, Australia (Conciliation and Arbitration Act), New Zealand.

[2] For example, Bahamas (Industrial Relations Act, s. 72); Bangladesh (Ordinance No. XXVI/1982, s. 8); Philippines (Labour Code, s. 273); Poland (Trade Union Law, 1982, s. 47 provides for sanctions against strike leaders); USSR (Penal Code of the RSFSR, s. 190).

In Japan, penal sanctions for strike action have been imposed by the Supreme Court on certain workers who have organised or instigated strikes in public services.

As regards the legislation in the USSR, the Committee on Freedom of Association has noted the formal assurance given by the Government of the USSR that a collective stoppage of work is not, and never has been regarded as absenteeism and that Soviet legislation does not provide, and never has provided any sanction in respect of a collective stoppage of work for the purpose of supporting the claims of the workers. The Committee has recommended the Government of the USSR to take appropriate steps to ensure that this assurance is generally known to the workers concerned (23rd Report, Case No. 111, para. 227). As regards section 190 of the Penal Code of the RSFSR mentioned above, the Government states that it does not share the Committee's opinion as concerns the interpretation given to this provision and the possibility of systematically applying penal sanctions in cases of strikes.

225.   The most common restrictions on the right of trade unions
to organise their activities and to formulate their programmes appear
to concern the political activities of organisations and the right to
strike.   Given the development of the trade union movement, union
action cannot nowadays be restricted solely to occupational matters.
A general prohibition of political activities is not only incompatible
with Convention No. 87 but it is also unrealistic for all practical
purposes.   Trade unions often undertake some measure of political
action, including support for a political party, which they may consider necessary for the advancement of their economic and social
objectives. Thus organisations should be able to make public their
views on a government's economic and social policy, provided that their
political action does not compromise the continuity of the union
movement or of its economic and social functions; governments, in turn,
must not endeavour to use organisations as political instruments.

226.   With regard to the right to strike, a general prohibition
- sometimes the result of express provisions or, as in many countries,
the cumulative effect of provisions concerning the official disputes
settlement machinery — constitutes a considerable limitation on the
means available to trade unions to further and defend the interests of
their members and on their right to organise their activities. A
prohibition of this nature can only be justified in circumstances of
acute national crisis and for a limited duration. A permanent ban on
strikes should only be imposed on public servants acting in their
capacity as public authority officials and on workers in essential
services, and should be compensated by the existence of adequate
impartial and speedy conciliation and arbitration procedures. Finally,
restrictions relating to the objectives of a strike and to the methods
used should be sufficiently reasonable as not to result in practice in
a total prohibition or an excessive limitation of the exercise of the
right to strike.

CHAPTER VIII

Dissolution and suspension
of organisations

227.   Article 4 of Convention No. 87 provides that workers' and
employers' organisations shall not be liable to be dissolved or
suspended by administrative authority. According to Article 6 of the
Convention,   this   provision   also   applies   to   federations   and
confederations. It is evident that suspension or dissolution of
occupational organisations by virtue of administrative powers does not
provide all the guarantees which normal judicial procedure alone can
ensure. The same principle applies to dissolution or suspension by law
or   by   decree: in   fact,   a   decree   suspending   or   dissolving   an
organisation constitutes an administrative measure contrary to Article
4 of the Convention and, moreover, a law to the same effect would be
incompatible with Article 8, paragraph 2, of the Convention according
to which the law of the land shall not be such as to impair, nor shall
it be so applied as to impair, the guarantees provided for in the
Convention.   Cancellation of registration may also have the same or a
similar result as suspension or dissolution, either because such
cancellation entails dissolution or because unregistered unions are
deprived of important advantages in the carrying out of their
occupational functions.

228.   In most countries, the dissolution of an organisation can
be declared only by the judicial authorities, when national legislation
has been contravened.   In some countries, the law provides that
cancellation of an organisation's registration has to be ordered by the
courts following a request from the registrar.[1]

229.   There are, however, a number of countries whose legislation
permits dissolution by administrative authority.[2] The situation   varies
according to the legal possibilities that exist of lodging an appeal
with the courts against the administrative decision and according to
the effects of the appeal.   It is in fact not always clear whether an

----

[1] For example, Pakistan (Industrial Relations Act).

[2] For example, Bolivia (Decree made under the General Labour Act,
s.   129); Colombia (Labour Code, s. 50 - dissolution of a trade union
which has organised or supported an unlawful strike); Guatemala (Labour
Code, s. 226 - however, the regulations for the implementation of
Conventions Nos. 87 and 98 which were adopted and published on 3
December 1981 stipulate that the provisions of paragraph (a) of s.   226
of   the Code concerning the dissolution of trade unions, when it can be
proved in court that they are involved in electoral or party politics,
are applied in the light of the guarantees provided under Article 43,
paragraph 4, and Articles 44 and 65 of the Constitution); Senegal (Act
No. 65-40/1965 - the Government states that these provisions are no
longer applied); Yemen (Labour Code, s. 157).

appeal is possible[1] and, even where it is, it does not necessarily have the effect of staying the execution of the administrative decision.[2]

230. As regards the suspension of organisations or of their activities, in certain countries suspension by administrative authority is specifically provided for in the legislation.[3]

231. Under the legislation of other countries, the registrar has more or less discretionary power to cancel the registration of a trade union.[4] There is generally a right of appeal against such a decision.

----

[1] For example, El Salvador (Labour Code, s. 230); Somalia (Labour Code, s. 27).

[2] For example, Venezuela (Labour Act, ss. 193-199 - the Government states that in practice this provision is hardly ever applied).

[3] For example, Colombia (Labour Code, s. 450); El Salvador (Labour Code, s. 230); Kenya (Trade Unions Ordinance, ss. 17 and 18); Malaysia (Trade Unions Act, s. 18).

In the case of Panama, the Committee noted with satisfaction in 1973 that the new Labour Code had repealed section 294 of the earlier Code which empowered the Minister of Labour to suspend trade unions by administrative action.

[4] For example, Ghana (Trade Unions Ordinance, s. 14); India (Trade Unions Act, ss. 10 and 11); Kenya (Trade Unions Ordinance, ss. 17 and 18); Malawi (Trade Unions Ordinance, ss. 13 and 14); New Zealand (Industrial Relations Act, s. 120); Sri Lanka (Trade Unions Ordinance, ss. 15-18).

In certain cases, some of the grounds for cancellation listed in the legislation seem to give the registrar and minister more or less discretionary power when taking their decision.

This is the case, for example, in Malaysia (if the registrar considers that a union has been, is being, or is likely to be used for unlawful purposes or for any purpose contrary to its rules: Trade Unions Act, s. 15); Singapore (if he considers that a union is being used against the interests of the workers or, having regard to the existence of another union for the same category of workers, he considers that it is necessary in the interests of the workers to deregister a union: Trade Unions Ordinance, s. 15).

In the case of Guyana, the Committee noted with satisfaction in 1973 that section 27 of the Trade Unions Ordinance had been amended, to the effect that a decision of the registrar to withdraw or cancel the registration of a trade union shall not apply until the time allowed for the filing of an appeal to the High Court has expired or, where such an appeal has been filed, until the appeal has been determined by the High Court.

Similarly, in the case of Japan, the Committee noted with satisfaction in 1979 that a provision had been introduced in Act No. 79 of 1978 to the effect that the cancellation of the registration of a trade union can take effect only after the expiry of the period for appeal or after the decision of the court if an appeal has been lodged.

It can, however, in some cases, only be brought before the competent minister.[1] In cases where a decision to cancel an organisation's registration, even though open to appeal to the judicial authorities, may take effect before the judicial authorities have given their decision or even before an appeal has been lodged, the legislation has the effect of permitting the suspension of a trade union by administrative authority.

232. The proper implementation of the principle set out in Article 4 of the Convention implies more than the existence of a legislative provision providing for the possibility of appealing against such decisions to the courts; decisions should not be permitted to take effect until a specified period of time has elapsed without any appeal being lodged or until they have been confirmed by the judicial authority. However, even a right of appeal to the courts does not always constitute a sufficient guarantee since, if the authority possesses discretionary power in reaching its decision, the judges can do no more than verify whether the law has been correctly applied. The judges should therefore be in a position to examine the substance of the case as well as the grounds for the dissolution or suspension of an organisation.

233. Apart from the cases where the dissolution or suspension of a trade union is governed by ordinary trade union legislation, there are a number of instances in which trade unions have been dissolved or suspended by ad hoc legislation, by a special act or decree.[2]

234. The Committee on Freedom of Association, which has examined a number of cases of dissolution or suspension of one or more trade unions or of the suspension of their activities, has recalled on many occasions that trade union organisations should not be dissolved by administrative authority and has emphasised the particular gravity of a measure providing for the suspension of trade union activities which

----

[1] For example, Malaysia (Trade Unions Act, s. 71A); Singapore (Trade Unions Act, ss. 17 and 18: the minister's decision is final and no appeal to the courts is possible).

[2] For example, Central African Republic (the General Union of Central African Workers (UGTC) was dissolved by Presidential Decree of 16 May 1981; moreover, since 1 September 1981 the activities of trade union organisations have been suspended); Nigeria (the registration of all trade unions was cancelled by Decree No. 22 of 1978, which amounted to dissolution by administrative authority); Poland (the registration of all existing trade unions was cancelled under the Trade Union Act of 8 October 1982); Turkey (after the military takeover of 12 September 1980, certain trade unions were suspended).

In Tanzania, the President of the Republic may order the cancellation of the registration of a trade union, subject to the approval of the National Executive Committee of the Party (Trade Union Ordinance, Chpt. 381 and JUWATA Act, 1979).

In the case of Greece, the Committee noted with satisfaction in 1977 the enactment of Act No. 89 of 1975 which restored full rights to the trade unions dissolved under the previous regime and provided for the restitution, as far as possible, of their property.

affects all aspects of trade union life.[1] The Committee cn Freedcm of
Association considers that it is essential that any dissolution or
suspension of workers' or employers' organisations should be carried
out in the final event by the judicial authorities, which alone can
guarantee the rights of defence. These principles, the Committee has
pointed out, are equally applicable when such measures of suspension or
dissolution are taken even during an emergency situation.[2] The
Committee on Freedom of Association has also recalled the principle
that the assets of dissolved trade unions should be temporarily placed
in trust and finally distributed amonq the members of the dissolved
organisation or transferred to the organisation which succeeds it, it
being understood that this expression means the organisation which
continues the aims for which the first organisation was set up and does
so in the same spirit.[3]

*   *   *

235. The dissolution and suspension of trade union organisations
are extreme forms of interference by the authorities in the activities
of organisations. In view of the gravity of these measures, therefore,
it is important that they should be accompanied by all the necessary
guarantees, which can only be secured under normal judicial procedure.

---

[1] ILO: Committee on Freedom of Association, 214th Report, Cases
Nos. 1040 and 1097, paras. 603 and 751.

[2] ILO: Committee on Freedom of Association, 220th Report, Cases
Nos. 997, 999 and 1029, para. 86.

[3] ILO: Committee on Freedom of Association, 110th Report, Case No.
519, para. 82; 194th Report, Case No. 900, para. 258; 221st Report,
Case No. 1097, para. 87.

CHAPTER IX

Right of organisations to establish and join federations and confederations and to affiliate with international organisations

236. Article 5 of Convention No. 87 provides that "workers' and employers' organisations shall have the right to establish and join federations and confederations and any such organisation, federation or confederation shall have the right to affiliate with international organisations of workers and employers". Article 6 stipulates that the provisions of Articles 2, 3 and 4 of the Convention apply to federations and confederations.

237. Convention No. 87, therefore, does not merely recognise the right of organisations to establish bodies operating at a higher level; it extends to the latter the same rights as are accorded to the first-level organisations.

Right of federation and confederation

238. In order to co-ordinate, standardise and centralise their activities, to carry more weight and to secure better protection for the workers, trade unions generally group together in federations - either federations with a vertical structure covering organisations which represent the same or similar categories of workers or federations with a horizontal structure which operate on a geographical basis and consist of trade unions representing workers in different occupations or branches of activity. In the same desire to standardise their activities and increase the protection they afford, trade union federations in turn often form national and inter-occupational confederations.

239. In many countries, trade unions are able to exercise the right of federation and confederation in complete freedom. Elsewhere, however, the right is curtailed by a number of legal <u>restrictions</u>.

Minimum number of member organisations

240. Certain legislative provisions governing the creation of federations and confederations stipulate - normally for both types of organisation - a minimum requirement for the number of member organisations; this may be expressed either as a fixed number or as a proportion of the lower-level organisations.[1] In so far as they require the affiliation of a large number of organisations, provisions such as
----

[1] For example, Brazil (Consolidated Labour Laws, ss. 534 and 535); Colombia (Decree No. 1469/1978, ss. 27 and 28); Dominican Republic (Resolution No. 15/1964); El Salvador (Labour Code, s. 257); Philippines (Labour Code, s. 237a); Portugal (Legislative Decree No. 215 B/75).

these are liable to prevent the establishment of federations and confederations.

Limited affiliation

241. In certain countries, many of which also stipulate a minimum membership of the kind described above, the law only allows organisations of the same profession, branch of activity or region to group together in federations or confederations. In this case, it is impossible to form inter-occupational or inter-regional associations.

242. In most of the countries involved, the legislation requires member organisations to belong to the same branch of activity or occupation.[1] In some others, legislative provisions imposing occupational restrictions are found side by side with requirements as to the geographical origin of these federations or confederations.[2]

243. The most serious problem arises under the single-trade-union system, where only one federation may be constituted for a given occupation (or groups thereof) or region and where not more than one national centre or confederation of workers or employers is admitted. This situation has already been examined and commented upon in the section on trade union monopoly in Chapter V. It should be added that in certain countries a national confederation or trade union has been set up by legislation.[3]

244. While in some cases the law authorises the formation only of a single central organisation for the whole country, the opposite situation arises in one country whose legislation prohibits the establishment of a national confederation covering the workers of different branches of activity and lists the confederations that may legally exist, which correspond to specific economic activities.[4] In another country trade union legislation does not apply to confederations,[5] while elsewhere again the legislation contains no provisions regarding the right to establish federations and confederations.[6]

245. The guarantees provided for by the Convention imply that organisations must be entitled to form federations freely if they so wish, as regards both the occupations and the geographical area that they cover. Consequently, legislation requiring an excessive minimum number of trade unions or federations for the establishment of organisations of a higher level or preventing the formation of federations composed of unions which represent different activities is

----

[1] For example, Kuwait (Labour Act, 1964, s. 79); Malaysia (Trade Unions Act, ss. 72 and 73); Peru (Supreme Decree No. 021, s. 23).

[2] For example, Nicaragua (Trade Union Regulations, ss. 43 and 62); Philippines (Labour Code, ss. 237 and 238).

[3] For example, Kenya, Tanzania, Uganda, Zambia.

[4] Brazil (Consolidated Labour Laws, s. 535).

[5] Argentina (Act No. 22105/1979 — according to the Government, confederations could be established under ordinary civil law).

[6] Ghana.

incompatible with the provisions of the Convention. Similarly, prohibition of the establishment of federations or a requirement that previous authorisation be obtained are clearly contrary to the principle of freedom to create organisations of a higher level. Finally, confederations should be able to represent lower-level organisations belonging to different branches and occupations and to operate at the national level. The Committee also must recall that legislation which authorises the establishment of only one confederation for a particular occupation or region or only a single national confederation or centre is contrary to the provisions of the Convention.

Limitation of the right to federate and confederate of specific categories of trade unions

246. Legislation sometimes contains specific provisions regarding the right of certain types of workers' organisation to form federations and confederations. In several countries, for example, organisations of public servants and of agricultural workers[1] are explicitly or implicitly required by law to federate among themselves and are prevented from affiliating respectively with private sector federations or federations of non-agricultural workers. Therefore, in the case of public sector trade unions and agricultural workers' trade unions, these provisions subject the right of federation to restrictions that are not imposed on the other organisations.

247. Restrictions on public sector organisations often take the form of a formal prohibition of affiliation with other organisations.[2] Sometimes a prohibition of affiliation with private sector trade unions may ensue indirectly from provisions preventing public servants from belonging to organisations that envisage or impose the use of strike action.[3]

248. For the Convention to be properly applied, organisations of public sector officials should have the right to affiliate with federations and confederations whose membership includes private sector organisations. Any restriction in this respect is incompatible with the right of organisations to establish and join federations and

----

[1] See Chapter XIII on rural workers.

[2] For example, Malaysia (Trade Unions Act, s. 27 - with regard to workers in public bodies, their trade unions may affiliate only with unions whose affiliation is likewise restricted to workers in the public sector); Mexico (Federal Law for Workers in the Service of the State, s. 79; however, the Federation of State Employees is a member of the Labour Congress, to which trade unions covering other types of employees also belong); Peru (Decree No. 063/82 PCM, s. 18).

In the case of Cyprus, the Committee noted with satisfaction in 1981 that section 59(1) of the Public Service Law, which restricted the rights of civil servants to join trade unions, had been repealed by Law No. 31/1980.

[3] For example, Switzerland (Federal Act respecting the Conditions of Service of Federal Employees, 1927).

confederations of their own choosing, unless affiliation to the higher-level body is linked to the obligation to use strike action.[1]

249. As to **the activities of higher-level organisations**, a number of countries impose certain important restrictions on their activities which deny them the right to strike or to bargain collectively, or both.[2] Restrictions of this type can seriously hamper the development of industrial relations, particularly in the case of small unions which, on account of their limited strength and untrained leadership, may not be able by themselves to further and defend in an effective manner the interests of their members. Provisions of this nature are incompatible with Article 5 of the Convention.[3]

International affiliation

250. The right of workers' and employers' organisations to affiliate with international occupational organisations seems to be recognised in most countries. There are, however, several exceptions, as when national legislation makes the affiliation subject to previous authorisation by the public authorities[4] or only permits affiliation under certain conditions fixed by law.[5] Sometimes, the law prohibits trade unions from receiving financial assistance or subsidies from occupational organisations outside the country.[6] The Committee on Freedom of Association considers that prohibitions of this nature are prejudicial to the guarantees provided for in Article 5 of the Convention, in as much as the principle of free affiliation to international organisations implies the right for national trade unions

----

[1] See para. 214 above.

[2] For example, Chile (Legislative Decree No. 2758/1979, ss. 4 and 7); Colombia (Labour Code, s. 417); Ecuador (Labour Code, s. 457); El Salvador (Labour Code, s. 260); Honduras (Labour Code, s. 537); Swaziland (Industrial Relations Act, 1980, s. 33); Uruguay (Act No. 15328 of 1982, s. 2).

[3] See ILO: Committee on Freedom of Association, 217th Report, Case No. 1109, para. 483.

[4] For example, Bahamas (Industrial Relations Act, s. 38); Brazil (Consolidated Labour Laws, s. 565); Kenya (Presidential Decision, 1965); Libyan Arab Jamahiriya (Act No. 107/1975, ss. 19, 28 and 29); Malawi (Trade Union Ordinance, s. 34); Malaysia (information supplied by the Government); Swaziland (Industrial Relations Act, 1980, s. 34); Zambia (Industrial Relations Act, s. 119).

[5] In Ethiopia (Proclamation No. 222 of 1982), the law only allows the sole central organisation the right to sign agreements with international organisations on the basis of the principles of proletarian internationalism. In Chad, trade unions may affiliate with African-aligned organisations.

[6] For example, Argentina (Act No. 22105/1979, s. 10); Philippines (Labour Code, s. 271 - previous authorisation must be obtained from the minister); Zambia (Industrial Relations Act); Zimbabwe (Act concerning unlawful organisations).

to benefit from the services and advantages flowing from their affiliation.[1]

251. Provisions such as these are not compatible with the principles of free and voluntary affiliation of trade unions with international organisations guaranteed under Article 5 of the Convention. The latter gives expression to the fact that workers or employers are united by a solidarity of interests, a solidarity which is not limited either to one specific undertaking or industry or even to the national economy but extends to the whole international economy. The right corresponds in fact to the practice followed by the United Nations and the International Labour Organisation, both of which have formally recognised international organisations of workers and employers by granting them consultative status and, in the case of the ILO, associating them directly with its activities.[2] The principles set forth in Article 5 carry with them the right of national trade unions to benefit from the advantages and services which may result from their affiliation, the right for representatives of the trade unions to participate in the work of the international organisations with which their unions are affiliated and the right for national and international organisations to keep contact with one another and to exchange their trade union publications.

*
* *

252. In order to defend the interests of their members more effectively, the first-level trade unions must have the right to form federations and confederations of their own choosing. Moreover, if this right is not to remain a dead letter, the higher-level organisations must also enjoy the rights accorded to the basic organisations, including the right to bargain collectively and to strike. It is also an important feature of the international solidarity of workers and employers that national federations and confederations should be able to unite at the international level without hindrance.

----

[1] See ILO: Committee on Freedom of Association, 201st Report, Case No. 842, para. 58.

[2] See ILO: Committee on Freedom of Association, 181st Report, Case No. 880, para. 113.

The right to organise
and collective bargaining

Introduction

253. The Right to Organise and Collective Bargaining Convention, 1949 (No. 98), deals with two essential aspects of trade union rights: workers' exercise of their right to organise vis-à-vis employers - the Convention contains specific provisions for the protection of the individual worker against acts of anti-union discrimination and for the protection of workers' and employers' organisations against interference in each other's affairs - and the promotion of voluntary collective bargaining (Articles 1 to 4).

254. As in the case of Convention No. 87, this instrument permits member States to determine the extent to which the guarantees provided for in the Convention shall apply to the armed forces and the police (Article 5).

255. With regard to public servants, who are covered without distinction by Convention No. 87, Article 6 of Convention No. 98 establishes that the Convention does not deal with the position of public servants engaged in the administration of the State, nor shall it be construed as prejudicing their rights or status in any way. The Committee considers that, while the concept of public servant may vary to some degree under the various national legal systems, the exclusion from the scope of the Convention of persons who are employed by the State or in the public sector, but who do not act as agents of the public authority (even though they may be in a situation identical with that of public officials engaged in the administration of the State) is contrary to the meaning of the Convention; the Committee also considers that this is made even clearer in the English text of Article 6 of the Convention, which permits the exclusion solely of public servants "engaged in the administration of the State". The Committee could not admit the exclusion from the terms of the Convention of important categories of workers employed by the State merely on the grounds that they are formally assimilated to public officials engaged in the administration of the State. If this were the case, the Convention might be deprived of much of its scope. The distinction therefore must be drawn between, on the one hand, public servants who by their functions are directly engaged in the administration of the State - that is, civil servants employed in government ministries and other comparable bodies, as well as officials acting as supporting elements in these activities - and, on the other hand, other persons employed by the government, by public undertakings or by autonomous public institutions. Only the former category can be excluded from the scope of the Convention.

CHAPTER X

Protection against acts
of anti-union discrimination

256.   An important aspect of the right to organise is the protection afforded to workers and trade union leaders against acts of anti-union discrimination and victimisation by the employer. Discrimination on grounds of trade union membership or activities can take several forms.   Article 1 of Convention No. 98 establishes first of all in general terms that "workers shall enjoy adequate protection against acts of anti-union discrimination in respect of their employment".   It then provides that such protection shall apply more particularly in respect of acts calculated to: "(a) make the employment of a worker subject to the condition that he shall not join a union or shall relinquish trade union membership; (b) cause the dismissal cf or otherwise prejudice a worker by reason of union membership or because of participation in union activities outside working hours or, with the consent of the employer, within working hours".   It follows from these provisions that workers must be adequately protected against anti-union discrimination both at the time of taking up employment and in the course of their employment relationship.[1]

257.   As regards union security clauses, which have the effect of making union membership, or payment of union contributions compulsory, the Committee on Industrial Relations at the 32nd Session of the International Labour Conference finally agreed to express the view in its report that Convention No. 98 could in no way be interpreted as

----

[1] The Committee recalls that, as regards public servants in particular, Article 4 of the Labour Relations (Public Service) Convention, 1978 (No. 151) stipulates that:

"1.   Public employees shall enjoy adequate protection against acts of anti-union discrimination in respect of their employment.

2.   Such protection shall apply more particularly in respect of acts calculated to -

(a)   make the employment of public employees subject to the condition that they shall not join or shall relinquish membership of a public employees' organisation;

(b)   cause the dismissal of or otherwise prejudice a public employee by reason of membership of a public employees' organisation or because of participation in the normal activities of such organisation."

authorising or prohibiting union security clauses, such questions being matters for regulation in accordance with national practice.[1]

258. In most countries, the legislation contains general or detailed provisions protecting workers against acts of anti-union discrimination. However, the extent of protection varies according to the period covered, the persons protected and the procedures for enforcing the protective provisions.

The period covered and persons protected

259. In a number of cases the legislation contains provisions aimed at protecting workers covered by the labour law against acts of anti-union discrimination, both at the time of taking up employment and in the course of employment;[2] in other countries, while the legislation

----

[1] ILO: Record of Proceedings, ILC, 32nd Session, 1949, p. 468. See also above, paras. 142 to 145.

[2] For example, Argentina (Act No. 22105, ss. 55 to 60); Austria (Act of 14 December 1973); Belgium (Act of 24 May 1921); Benin (Labour Code, s. 7); Brazil (Penal Code, s. 199, and Consolidated Labour Laws, s. 543); Byelorussian SSR (Labour Code and Penal Code); Canada (Canadian Labour Code, Part V, Criminal Code and provincial legislation); Chad (Labour Code, s. 37); Chile (Legislative Decree No. 2756/1979, s. 4); Comoros (Labour Code, s. 42); Congo (Labour Code, s. 210); Djibouti (Act No. 56.416 of 1956, s. 1(a)); Dominican Republic (Labour Code, s. 307; the Committee considers, however, that these provisions are inadequate); France (Labour Code, Book IV, s. L.412-2); Federal Republic of Germany (Works Councils Act, 1972, s. 75; Act of 25 August 1969; Constitution, art. 9(3); Civil Code, s. 134); Greece (Act No. 1264 of 1982, ss. 14 and 15); Grenada (Act No. 29/1979, s. 7); Haiti (Labour Code, s. 265); Italy (Act No. 300 of 1970, ss. 15 and 16); Ivory Coast (Labour Code, s. 4(1) and (2)); Japan (Trade Union Law, s. 7); Jordan (Labour Code, s. 79); Luxembourg (Act of 11 May 1936, s. 4); Malaysia (Industrial Relations Act); Mali (Labour Code, ss. 68 and 306); Mauritania (Labour Code, Book I, s. 63; Book III, ss. 3 and 26); Mexico (Constitution, Art. 123 and Federal Labour Law, s. 357); Nicaragua (Decree No. 790, s. 191); Niger (Labour Code, s. 4); Pakistan (Industrial Relations Ordinance, s. 15); Panama (Labour Code, s. 388); Papua New Guinea (Industrial Organisations Act, s. 66); Paraguay (Labour Code, ss. 65 and 282); Peru (Decree 009 of 1961, ss. 2 and 4); Philippines (Labour Code, ss. 249 and 250); Poland (Trade Union Act, 1982, s. 4); Portugal (Legislative Decrees 215/B/75 and 164/A/76); Senegal (Labour Code, s. 29); Somalia (Labour Code, s. 15); Spain (Act of 10 March 1980 and Decree No. 342/79); Swaziland (Industrial Relations Act, 1980, s. 70); Togo (Labour Code, s. 4); Trinidad and Tobago (Industrial Relations Act, 1972, s. 42); Uganda (Trade Unions Decree, s. 29); Ukrainian SSR (Labour Code and Penal Code); USSR (Russian SFSR: Labour Code and Penal Code); United Kingdom (Employment Acts, 1980 and 1982 and Employment Protection Acts, 1975 and 1978); United States (Labor-Management Relations Act, ss. 7 and 8; from the texts of the laws and other reports submitted by the Government, the Committee notes that various categories of workers covered by Conventions Nos. 87, 98 and 141 are excluded from the protection of federal law and that there is no legislative protection of the rights addressed in these Conventions in a number of States); Uruguay (Decree No. 622 of 1973); Venezuela (Labour Code, ss. 168 and 169); Zaire (Labour Code, s. 228); Zambia (Industrial Relations Act, s. 4); Zimbabwe (Industrial Conciliation Act and Employment Regulations No.
(Footnote continued on next page)

specifically protects workers against victimisation, particularly
dismissal, during their employment, it does not seem to contain
measures of protection applicable to their engagement;[1] in some
countries there are not even any legal provisions protecting workers
against acts of anti-union discrimination:[2] in the event of dismissal,
for example, the employer is usually not bound to give reasons for
effecting the dismissal.[3]

(Footnote continued from previous page)

894 of 1981, s. 6). Most of the French non-metropolitan territories
apply the same legislation as in France.

As regards Barbados, the Committee noted with satisfaction in
1975 that the text amending the Trade Unions Act (1974) contains a new
provision to prevent acts calculated to cause the dismissal of or
otherwise prejudice a worker or to bring pressure on him by reason of
his trade union membership, functions or activities.

It also noted with satisfaction in 1977 that in Dominica the
Industrial Relations Act adopted in 1975 provides for protection of
workers against acts of anti-trade union discrimination at the time of
engagement.

In 1977, it also noted with satisfaction the new legislative
provisions in Portugal which took account of its comments on the lack
of specific provisions against acts of anti-union discrimination.

It noted with satisfaction in 1973 that the Industrial Relations
Act of 1972 in Trinidad and Tobago provides specific protection against
acts of anti-union discrimination at the time of engagement of a
worker.

[1] For example, Australia (for members of registered unions);
Democratic Yemen (Act No. 24 of 1981); Ecuador; Finland; Ghana; Libyan
Arab Jamahiriya (Act No. 107/1975, s. 14); Netherlands (the Government
and the Labour Foundation plan to draw up a code of good conduct on
this point).

[2] For example, Cape Verde, Gabon, Guinea-Bissau, Indonesia,
Lebanon, Sri Lanka, Switzerland, Yemen. The Committee of Experts has
requested the Government of Costa Rica to lay down explicitly in the
legislation remedies and sanctions to ensure the effective application
of Article 1 of the Convention.

[3] For example, Switzerland. This Government indicates that there
is justification for the legal concept whereby the law concerning
termination of contract on grounds of military service or civil service
- based on the principle that such dismissal is a clear abuse of the
law on dismissals - could also apply by analogy, to the jurisprudence
of the courts, in particular as concerns the juridical effect on other
cases of violation of the law on dismissals, notably in the case of
dismissal on grounds of union membership or union activities. The
worker who is a victim of an act of anti-union discrimination can
prosecute his employer before the civil courts for violation of the law
(Civil Code, s. 2(2)), for damages to his personal interests (Civil
Code, s. 28) or for omission to fulfil the general obligation of
protection (Code of Obligations, s. 328(1)). The burden of proof that
he was a victim of anti-union discrimination falls on the worker. Many
collective agreements set up bodies having competence to hear this type
of dispute.

260. It must be emphasised that the protection provided for in Article 1 of the Convention covers not only dismissal but also any other discriminatory measure which might arise in the course of employment, in particular transfers, refusal of advancement, demotions, disciplinary measures, deprivation of or limitations on wages or social benefits and other prejudicial acts.[1]

261. In contrast to legislation which protects workers only partially or not at all against acts of anti-union discrimination, some legislation provides special protection to certain members of a union. Thus, special protection against dismissal or other acts of discrimination is sometimes afforded to members of a union which has applied for registration or which is in the process of formation[2] or to the founding members of a trade union.[3] Such protection may also be afforded against dismissals aimed at substantially reducing the proportion of unionised workers or of members of a particular union among the workers in an enterprise.[4]

262. The legislation in a large number of countries emphasises special protection of trade union representatives,[5] who are usually more exposed to acts of discrimination.[6]

----

[1] For example, in Greece, justification for the transfer of an elected member of a trade union is determined by a special tripartite committee (the president of the court of first instance, a workers' representative and an employers' representative) (Trade Union Act of 1982, ss. 14 and 15).

[2] For example, Australia (Commonwealth Conciliation and Arbitration Act, s. 5); New Zealand (Industrial Relations Act, s. 15C); Nicaragua (Decree No. 790, ss. 192-193).

[3] For example, Colombia (Labour Code, s. 406), Ecuador (Labour Code, s. 188); Guatemala (Labour Code, s. 223); Honduras (Labour Code, s. 517); New Zealand (Industrial Relations Act, s. 150); Panama (Labour Code, ss. 381, 383, 384); Peru (Decree No. 23-DT57 and Decree No. 27/57); Sweden (Act 506/36); Venezuela (Labour Code, s. 198 and Decree 1563/73, s. 358).

[4] For example, El Salvador (Labour Code, s. 251); Panama (Labour Code, s. 388).

[5] For example, Algeria, Angola, Argentina, Brazil, Colombia, Ecuador, Egypt, Finland, France, Guatemala, Honduras, Hungary, India, Italy, Nicaragua, Pakistan, Panama, Peru, Romania, Spain, Trinidad and Tobago, USSR, Venezuela. In Egypt (Act No. 1/1981, s. 48) and in Brazil (Codification of Labour Law, s. 543) the law also protects candidates for election to the executive committee of a trade union organisation during the period of their candidacy.

[6] The Workers' Representatives Convention (No. 135) and Recommendation (No. 143) of 1971 provide that workers' representatives (including trade union representatives) in the undertaking are to enjoy effective protection against any act prejudicial to them, including dismissal, based on their status or activities as a workers' representative or on union membership or participation in union activities, in so far as they act in conformity with existing laws or collective agreements or other jointly agreed arrangements. The Recommendation provides that measures which should be taken to ensure effective protection might include, inter alia, in respect of the unjustified termination of employment of the representatives, provision for an effective remedy
(Footnote continued on next page)

263. Such protection is particularly desirable, because in order to be able to perform their trade union duties in full independence, trade union officers and representatives must have the guarantee that they will not be prejudiced on account of the trade union mandate which they hold. The guarantee of such protection in the case of union officers is also necessary in order to ensure compliance with the essential principle that workers' organisations have the right to elect their representatives in full freedom. One of the ways of ensuring protection of representatives is to provide that they may not be dismissed either during their term of office or for a specified period following its expiry except, of course, in the event of a serious offence.

Enforcement procedures

264. Under the terms of Article 3 of Convention No. 98, machinery appropriate to national conditions must be established, where necessary, for the purpose of ensuring respect for the right to organise. The effectiveness of legal provisions governing protection of workers and trade union representatives depends to a large extent on the way in which these provisions are applied in practice. In fact, experience shows that the existence of basic legal standards prohibiting acts of anti-union discrimination is not enough if they are not accompanied by effective procedures to ensure their application in practice.

265. These procedures and machinery to enforce the prohibition of anti-union discrimination may take the form of prevention, or compensation, or they may entail penal sanctions.

266. The rules existing in some countries (which sometimes also protect candidates for trade union office or union leaders during specified periods after their term has expired) provide that certain measures (such as dismissals or transfers) taken against trade union representatives must first be authorised by an independent body or public authority: thus, the labour inspectorate or industrial tribunals play an important part in the prevention of acts of anti-union discrimination.[1] Sometimes this authorisation is obtained from the

----

(Footnote continued from previous page)

which, unless this is contrary to basic principles of the law of the country concerned, shall include the reinstatement of such representatives in their job with payment of unpaid wages and the maintenance of their acquired rights. The Recommendation also lays down the principle that the effective protection referred to above should under certain conditions equally apply to workers who are candidates for election or appointment; and might apply to workers who have ceased to be workers' representatives.

[1] For example, Brazil (Consolidated Labour Laws, s. 543); Chile (Legislative Decree No. 2756/78, s. 28, and Legislative Decree No. 2200, s. 22); Colombia (Labour Code, ss. 405 to 413); Egypt (Trade Union Act, s. 48); France (Labour Code, Book IV, s. L.412-15); Guatemala (Labour Code, s. 223); Honduras (Labour Code, s. 516); India (Industrial Disputes Act, s. 33); Panama (Labour Code, s. 383); Venezuela (Labour Code, s. 198).

In the Netherlands, authorisation must be obtained from the director of the regional employment office (government information: Extraordinary (Employment Relations) Decree, 1945, s. 6, and instructions to be observed by directors of employment offices).

trade union organisation[1] or from the works council.[2]

267.   In most legislation, however, the emphasis is laid not on prevention but on compensation: the latter should aim to compensate fully, both in financial and occupational terms, for the prejudice suffered by workers as a result of an act of anti-union discrimination. The bodies traditionally called upon to rule on cases of alleged discrimination have been the ordinary courts (civil and criminal), but in many countries the legislation now confers such powers on more specialised bodies, such as labour courts and industrial tribunals. Some legislation provides in particular that the employer's action must be suspended until the competent authority has ruled on the matter.

268.   Whatever the machinery available, the procedure of compensation for prejudice encounters certain problems, chiefly as a result of excessively lengthy proceedings, difficulties relating to the burden of proof, and the possibility for the employer to acquit himself by paying compensation. The Committee emphasises the necessity of providing expeditious, inexpensive and impartial means of redressing grievances caused by acts of anti-union discrimination as quickly as possible.

269.   In particular, placing on workers the burden of proving that the act in question occurred as a result of anti-union discrimination may constitute an insurmountable obstacle to compensation for the prejudice suffered. Therefore, some legislation places on the employer the onus of proving that the act of alleged anti-union discrimination was unconnected with trade union matters.[3]

270.   A number of countries have established special procedures for the investigation and determination of cases of anti-union discrimination. Bodies set up under these procedures have quasi-judicial competence to deal with such cases, and sometimes also with the settlement of industrial disputes and other matters. In some of these countries the effectiveness of these procedures would seem to be the result of the experience of the special bodies in dealing with these specific cases and in cases where circumstantial evidence plays an important role in the determination of the actual intentions of the employer.[4]

----

[1] For example, Algeria (Order No. 71-75, s. 10 - the dismissal must also be approved by the labour inspector); Hungary (Labour Code, s. 16); Romania (Labour Code, s. 132), USSR (Labour Code, s. 235).

[2] For example, Finland (Act No. 320, 1970, s. 53).

[3] For example, Australia, New Zealand.

In the United States, the National Labor Relations Board has just set a new precedent in a case of alleged violation of section 8(a)(3) of the Labor-Management Relations Act, with the Wright Line case (251 NLRB No. 150). The General Counsel must first establish a prima facie case sufficient to support the inference that trade union activity was a motivation in the employer's disciplinary action. Once this is established, the burden will shift to the employer to demonstrate that the same action would have taken place even in the absence of trade union activity on the part of the person concerned.

[4] For example, Canada, Ghana, Japan, Pakistan, Philippines, United States (the Committee notes, however, that the latest official report of the National Labor Relations Board, submitted by the Government,

(Footnote continued on next page)

271. The Committee on Freedom of Association has considered that it may often be difficult, if not impossible, for a worker to prove that he has been subjected to an act of anti-union discrimination. The Committee recalled that it is in this respect that Article 3 of Convention No. 98, concerning the establishment of the appropriate bodies for ensuring respect of the right to organise, acquires full significance.[1] In this connection, the Committee has pointed out that, in addition to protective machinery for preventing acts of anti-union discrimination (for example, requiring previous authorisation from the labour inspector before dismissing a union officer), a further means of ensuring effective protection would be to make it compulsory for the employer to prove that the motive for his intention to dismiss a worker has no connection with the worker's union activities.[2]

272. These questions have been dealt with in more recent international standards. Thus, the Workers' Representatives Recommendation, 1971 (No. 143), with a view to ensuring effective protection of workers' representatives, recommends, among the measures to be taken in the event of any alleged discriminatory dismissal or unfavourable change in the conditions of employment of a workers' representative, the adoption of provisions obliging the employer to prove that such action was justified.[3]

273. The Termination of Employment Convention, 1982 (No. 158) stipulates in Article 5 that the following, inter alia, do not constitute valid reasons for termination:

(a)   union membership or participation in union activities outside working hours or, with the consent of the employer, within working hours;

(b)   seeking office as, or acting or having acted in the capacity of, a workers' representative.[4]

(Footnote continued from previous page)

reveals a large and growing number of violations of the law which it administers, particularly by employers).

[1] See, for example, ILO: Committee on Freedom of Association, 214th Report, Case No. 1065, para. 421.

[2] See, for example, ILO: Committee on Freedom of Association, 217th Report, Case No. 1077, para. 428.

[3] See also paragraph 262 above, footnote 3.

[4] Article 9 of this Convention emphasises that "The bodies referred to in Article 8 of this Convention [an impartial body, such as a labour tribunal, etc.] shall be empowered to examine the reasons given for the termination and the other circumstances relating to the case and to render a decision on whether the termination was justified". As regards the onus of proof, Article 9 stipulates that "in order for the worker not to bear alone the burden of proving that the termination was not justified, the methods of implementation referred to in Article 1 of this Convention shall provide for one or the other or both of the following possibilities:

(a)   the burden of proving the existence of a valid reason for the termination as defined in Article 4 of this Convention shall rest on the employer;

(Footnote continued on next page)

274. A particular problem arises in connection with dismissals for economic reasons, which may have negative repercussions on unionised workers, and in particular on union officers in an undertaking, if they are used as an indirect means of subjecting them to acts of anti-union discrimination, under the guise of dismissal on economic grounds.

275. Convention No. 158 obliges the employer who is contemplating terminations for reasons of economic, technological, structural or similar nature, to consult with workers' representatives (Article 13) and to notify the competent authorities (Article 14).[1]

276. While these texts do not establish specific protection for unionised workers and union officers in the event of termination for economic reasons, it is to be hoped that they will help to protect them against acts of anti-union discrimination, in pursuance of the principle laid down by Convention No. 98.

277. As regards measures for compensating a unionised worker for prejudice suffered, the Committee considers that the reintegration and reinstatement in his post of a worker who has been dismissed or discriminated against for anti-union reasons constitute the most appropriate means of redressing acts of anti-union discrimination.[2] Legislation which includes protective provisions, but which allows the employer in practice to terminate the employment of a worker on condition that he pay the compensation provided for by law in all cases of unjustified dismissal, when the real motive is his trade union membership or activity, is inadequate under the terms of Article 1 of the Convention.

(Footnote continued from previous page)

(b)   the bodies referred to in Article 8 of this Convention shall be empowered to reach a conclusion on the reason for the termination having regard to the evidence provided by the parties and according to procedures provided for by national law and practice."

This Convention has not yet come into force.

[1] Article 13 provides that: "1. When the employer contemplates termination for reasons of an economic, technological, structural or similar nature, the employer shall:

(a)   provide the workers' representatives concerned in good time with relevant information including the reasons for the terminations contemplated, the number and categories of workers likely to be affected and the period over which the terminations are likely to be carried out."

Article 14 provides that: "1. When the employer contemplates termination for reasons of an economic, technological, structural or similar nature, he shall notify, in accordance with national law and practice, the competent authority thereof as early as possible, giving relevant information, including a written statement of the reasons for the terminations, the number of categories of workers likely to be affected and the period over which the terminations are intended to be carried out."

[2] Egypt (Trade Union Act No. 35 of 1976, as amended, s. 48); Nicaragua (Labour Code, s. 116).

278. In some countries the law provides for penal sanctions[1] (fines or prison, or both) to be imposed on employers who are guilty of anti-union discrimination. These sanctions should have a dual purpose, namely to punish the guilty and, above all, to act as a deterrent against such discrimination. It would be desirable for countries that have ratified Convention No. 98 to provide sanctions which would allow adequate protection against acts of discrimination.

*

* *

279. Article 1 of Convention No. 98 guarantees workers adequate protection against acts of anti-union discrimination both in taking up employment and in the course of employment and covers all measures of anti-union discrimination (dismissals, transfers, demotions and any other prejudicial acts). The protection provided in the Convention is particularly important in the case of trade union representatives and officers, as these must have the guarantee that they will not be prejudiced on account of the union mandate which they hold.

280. The effectiveness of legal provisions, however, depends to a large extent on the way in which these provisions are applied in practice and on the forms of compensation and sanctions provided. Legal standards are inadequate if they are not coupled with effective and expeditious procedures to ensure their application and with sufficiently dissuasive penal sanctions; machinery for preventive protection (for example, prior authorisation of the labour inspector in the event of dismissal) is particularly useful in this respect. The obligation of the employer to prove that there is no union-related motive underlying his intention to dismiss a worker or underlying the dismissal is an additional means of ensuring real protection of the right to organise as guaranteed by the Convention. Legislation which allows the employer in practice to terminate the employment of a worker on condition that he pays the compensation provided for by law in any case of unjustified dismissal, when the real motive is his union membership or activity, is inadequate under the terms of Article 1 of the Convention. Defective enforcement machinery is likewise inadequate. The reinstatement of the dismissed worker is obviously the most appropriate remedy in such cases of anti-union discrimination.

----

[1] For example, Algeria, Argentina, Australia, Austria, Bahamas, Belgium, Brazil, United Republic of Cameroon, Chad, Colombia, Ecuador, Egypt, Federal Republic of Germany, Finland, France, Greece, Grenada, Guatemala, Hungary, India, Italy, Japan, Malaysia, Mali, Mexico, New Zealand, Nicaragua, Pakistan, Panama, Peru, Philippines, Senegal, Spain, Tanzania, Trinidad and Tobago, USSR, Venezuela, Zambia, Zimbabwe.

CHAPTER XI

Protection against acts
of interference

281. Article 2 of Convention No. 98 establishes first in general terms that "workers' and employers' organisations shall enjoy adequate protection against any acts of interference by each other or each other's agents or members in their establishment, functioning or administration". The same Article goes on to describe particular acts of interference "which are designed to promote the establishment of workers' organisations under the domination of employers or employers' organisations, or to support workers' organisations by financial or other means, with the object of placing such organisations under the control of employers or employers' organisations". In order to make such protection effective, the same provision applies as in the case of acts of anti-union discrimination, namely, that machinery appropriate to national conditions must be established, where necessary, for the purpose of ensuring respect for the right to organise as defined in the preceding Articles (Article 3).[1], [2].

282. Several countries have adopted provisions aimed at protecting workers against acts of interference by employers.[3] Such

----

[1] As regards public servants more specifically, Article 5 of the Labour Relations (Public Service) Convention, 1978 (No. 151) lays down:

"1. Public employees' organisations shall enjoy complete independence from public authorities.

2. Public employees' organisations shall enjoy adequate protection against any acts of interference by a public authority in their establishment, functioning or administration."

[2] On the initiative of the Employers' group, the International Labour Conference decided to grant the same protection in this respect to employers' organisations as to workers' organisations (principle of equality of treatment). ILO: Record of Proceedings, IIC, 32nd Session, 1949, p. 468.

[3] For example, Argentina (Act No. 22105); Australia (Commonwealth Conciliation and Arbitration Act, Regulation 115); Austria (Act of 14 December 1973, s. 4); Brazil (Consolidated Labour Laws, s. 525); Burundi (Labour Code, s. 285); United Republic of Cameroon (Labour Code, s. 5); Canada (Canadian Labour Code, Part V); Chile (Legislative Decree No. 2356, s. 44); El Salvador (Labour Code, s. 205); Federal Republic of Germany (according to court decisions, only independent trade unions are protected by the Constitution and have the right to bargain collectively); Ghana (Industrial Relations Act, s. 27); Greece (Act No. 1264 of 1982, s. 14); Italy (Act No. 300 of 1970, s. 17); Japan (Trade Unions Act, ss. 2 and 7); Malaysia (Industrial Relations Act, s. 4); Mexico (Federal Labour Law, s. 133); Panama (Labour Code,

(Footnote continued on next page)

provisions are sometimes of a general nature but in other cases they
are more specific and may refer to the independence (i.e. the absence
of any control on the part of any employer) of a trade union as a
condition for its registration or otherwise, denial of bargaining
rights to a trade union which is not independent, prohibition of
financial or other support being given to a trade union by an employer
desirous of exerting control over it, forbidding employers to make
payments to trade union representatives, etc. The machinery set up to
enforce these provisions depends on the type of protection afforded by
the law, as well as on the various procedures established by national
law or practice: it may consist in the intervention of the Registrar of
trade unions or the labour administration, the labour courts or the
ordinary courts, or special bodies of the type referred to in Chapter
X, which are competent to deal with unfair labour practices such as
acts of anti-union discrimination and interference.

283. Specific protective provisions in the law are less frequent
with regard to acts of interference than to acts of anti-union
discrimination. Some governments consider, in this connection, that
the trade unions in their countries are sufficiently developed and
strong to protect these organisations against any acts of interference.
Nevertheless, governments which have ratified the Convention are under
the obligation to take specific action, in particular through
legislative means, to ensure respect for the guarantees laid down in
the Convention. In this respect, the Committee has had to make direct
requests and observations to governments wherever protection against
interference appears to be inadequate, particularly in the absence of
appropriate sanctions or where such acts have occurred in practice.[1]

(Footnote continued from previous page)

s. 388); Paraguay (Labour Code, s. 284); Peru (Decree 009 of 1961, s.
2); Philippines (Labour Code, ss. 248 and 249); Rwanda (Labour Code, s.
74); Somalia (Labour Code, s. 15); United Kingdom (Trade Unions and
Labour Relations Act, s. 3C); United States (Labor-Management
Relations Act and Labor-Management Reporting and Disclosure Act of
1959); Venezuela (Labour Code, s. 168); Zambia (Industrial Relations
Act).

In the case of Ecuador, the Committee noted with satisfaction in
1975 that section 43(j) of the new Labour Code prohibits an employer
from interfering in activities that are strictly union matters and from
violating the right to carry on such activities freely, and also that
the administrative authorities are careful to prevent such acts of
interference.

Similarly, in the case of Haiti, the Committee noted with
satisfaction in 1977 that as a result of direct contacts provisions
have been adopted on the protection of workers' organisations against
acts of interference by employers and their organisations (s. 265 of
the Labour Code).

In 1977 the Committee also noted with satisfaction that the new
legislation in Portugal, adopted in 1975 and 1976, took account of the
Committee's comments, especially on the lack of specific provisions
against acts of interference.

[1] Cape Verde, Colombia, Costa Rica, Dominican Republic, Gabon,
Guinea-Bissau, Indonesia, Ivory Coast, Jordan, Lebanon, Liberia,
Mauritius, Paraguay, Sri Lanka, Swaziland, Zaire.

284. The Committee on Freedom of Association has stressed on various occasions the need to adopt clear and precise provisions aimed at effectively protecting workers' organisations against acts of interference by employers and their organisations.[1] In particular, it has pointed out that to give the necessary publicity to provisions such as those of Article 2 of the Convention and ensure that full effect is given to them in practice, even in cases where ratification has the effect of incorporating the international standard in national law, it is highly important that these provisions, accompanied by provision for appeals and penalties to ensure that they are complied with, should be embodied explicitly in the relevant legislation.[2]

*

* * *

285. Article 2 of Convention No. 98 provides that workers' and employers' organisations should enjoy adequate protection against acts of interference by each other. It is important therefore that, whenever it appears that there is insufficient protection against interference or that such acts do occur in practice, governments take specific action, in particular through legislative means, to ensure that the guarantees provided for in the Convention are respected.

_____

[1] ILO: Committee on Freedom of Association, 181st Report, Cases Nos. 821, 859 and 875, para. 141.

[2] ILO: Committee on Freedom of Association, 197th Report, Cases Nos. 821, 859 and 875, para. 170.

CHAPTER XII

Promotion of
collective bargaining

286.   Article 4 of Convention No. 98 lays down that "measures appropriate to national conditions shall be taken, where necessary, to encourage and promote the full development and utilisation of machinery for voluntary negotiation between employers or employers' organisations and workers' organisations, with a view to the regulation of terms and conditions of employment by means of collective agreements".

287.   This Article deals with one of the most important aspects of industrial relations, namely, voluntary collective bargaining.

288.   Since Convention No. 98, the ILO has adopted a number of instruments relating to collective bargaining, of which the following are particularly worth noting.

289.   The Labour Relations (Public Service) Convention (No. 151) and Recommendation (No. 159) of 1978,[1] Article 7 of which provides that: "Measures appropriate to national conditions shall be taken, where necessary, to encourage and promote the full development and utilisation of machinery for negotiation of terms and conditions of employment between the public authorities concerned and public employees' organisations, or of such other methods as will allow representatives of public employees to participate in the determination of these matters".

290.   The Collective Bargaining Convention (No. 154) and Recommendation (No. 163) of 1981 which emphasise, inter alia, that: "Measures adapted to national conditions shall be taken to promote collective bargaining" (Article 5 of the Convention); such measures "shall not be so conceived or applied as to hamper the freedom of collective bargaining" (Article 8).[2]

291.   The main aspects of collective bargaining contemplated in Article 4 of Convention No. 98 are, on the one hand, governmental promotion of collective negotiation and, on the other hand, the voluntary character of the bargaining procedure and the autonomy of the bargaining parties.

----

[1] See also above paras. 14 and 20.

[2] Other instruments deal with particular aspects of bargaining: the Collective Agreements Recommendation, 1951 (No. 91); the Voluntary Conciliation and Arbitration Recommendation, 1951 (No. 92); the Examination of Grievances Recommendation, 1967 (No. 130); the Labour Administration Convention (No. 150) and Recommendation (No. 158), 1978.

Promotion

292. In the vast majority of countries the principle that workers have the right to participate in determining their conditions of employment through collective bargaining is recognised in law or applied in practice. Nevertheless, various kinds of restrictions on the freedom to conclude collective agreements exist in many countries.

Recognition of trade unions for the purposes of collective bargaining

293. Bargaining necessarily entails bargaining parties: on the one side, an employer or employers' organisation and, on the other side, one or more representative trade unions of workers.

294. The procedures for recognising the representative trade union(s) may be "voluntary", that is to say determined by a bipartite or tripartite agreement, or they may correspond to well-established practice; they may also be "compulsory", that is to say procedures for which statutory provision is made, and oblige the employer to recognise one or more trade unions under certain conditions. In this respect, workers in some countries may be represented by a number of trade unions even at the level of plant bargaining; other legislations, however, confer the exclusive right to bargain for a specific category of workers upon the organisation which represents a certain proportion or a relative or absolute majority of the workers, and whose representativity is generally determined either on the basis of the number of members (checking membership lists), or by secret ballot (checking number of votes).[1]

295. The Committee considers that, where systems provide for the most representative trade union to have preferential or exclusive bargaining rights, it is important that the determination of the trade union in question should be based on objective and pre-established criteria, so as to avoid any opportunity for partiality or abuse.[2] As regards legislation restricting recognition to an association which has

---

[1] For example, Bahamas (Industrial Relations Act, 1970, ss. 40 and 45); Canada (Canadian Labour Code, Part V); Costa Rica (Labour Code, s. 56); El Salvador (Labour Code, ss. 270 and 289); Honduras (Labour Code, s. 54); Mexico (Federal Labour Law, s. 388); Pakistan (Industrial Relations Ordinance, 1969); Philippines (Labour Code, ss. 234c and 237c); Singapore (Industrial Relations Act, 1971); Suriname (Decree E-28/1981); Trinidad and Tobago (Industrial Relations Act, 1972); United States (Labor-Management Relations Act).

[2] It has been suggested that where national legislation provides for a procedure of certifying unions as exclusive bargaining agents, certain safeguards should be attached, such as: (a) the certification to be made by an independent body; (b) the representative organisation to be chosen by a majority vote of the employees in the unit concerned; (c) the right of an organisation which fails to secure a sufficiently large number of votes to ask for a new election after a stipulated period; (d) the right of any organisation other than the certificated organisation to demand a new election after a reasonable period has elapsed (otherwise a majority of the workers concerned might belong to a union which, for an unduly long period, could be prevented from organising its administration and activities with a view to fully furthering and defending the interests of its members). (Committee on Freedom of Association, 109th Report, Case No. 533, para. 101.)

a membership or the support of more than 50 per cent of the persons in a given bargaining unit (absolute majority), it follows that a trade union, even with a majority, that does not cover 50 per cent of the persons in a unit cannot obtain a certificate as a recognised bargaining agent; the Committee has recalled that, if under a system of nominating an exclusive bargaining agent there is no union covering more than 50 per cent of the workers, collective bargaining rights should be granted to all the unions in this unit, at least on behalf of their own members.[1]

296.   There are close links between recognition of a trade union and the obligation to negotiate, since recognition often implies the obligation to negotiate with the trade union recognised as the bargaining agent. Numerous legal systems spell out this obligation in greater or lesser detail and, in some cases, decisions of the bodies responsible for administering the recognition procedures have specified exactly what the obligation involves. Refusal by an employer to recognise the designated or representative trade union and, sometimes, the fact that an employer bargains with another trade union or does not bargain in good faith with the agent granted the exclusive right to bargain (an attitude that is sometimes regarded as an unfair labour practice)[2] may give rise to special proceedings for damages or the application of sanctions.[3] The Committee stresses the importance which it attaches to the principle that employers should, for the purposes of collective bargaining, recognise the organisations which are representative of the workers they employ.

297.   As has already been indicated in Chapter IX on the right of employers' and workers' organisations to establish federations and confederations,[4] the right to bargain collectively should also be granted to federations and confederations since this right is not an exclusive prerogative of first-level organisations. Any restriction or prohibition in this regard may constitute an obstacle to the development of industrial relations. On the other hand, in one country trade unions have the right to conclude collective agreements at the national level covering all the workers in a given branch of industry. This provision seems to fix definitively the level of collective bargaining at industry level. This question ought normally to be left to the parties involved in the bargaining. Therefore the trade unions ought to be able, if they so wish, to negotiate at the level of the undertaking.[5]

----

[1] Trinidad and Tobago (Education Act, as amended, s. 74D).

[2] Countries in which there are provisions prohibiting certain practices regarded as prejudicial to collective bargaining include the following: Antigua and Barbuda, Canada, Dominican Republic, Ghana, Grenada, Jamaica, Japan, Malaysia, Pakistan, Panama, Philippines, Singapore, Spain, Suriname, Thailand, Trinidad and Tobago, United Kingdom, United States, Zambia.

[3] For example, Grenada (Act No. 29/1979); Suriname (Decree No. E-28/1981).

[4] See above, para. 249.

[5] Poland, Trade Union Act, 1982, s. 23.

Machinery and procedures to facilitate bargaining

298. Collective bargaining can be carried on either very informally or within a more or less elaborate institutional and procedural framework.

299. Many countries have an established conciliation procedure or machinery for the furtherance of collective bargaining. Conciliation is often compulsory and workers' and employers' organisations are under an obligation to appear and participate in the proceedings or in the machinery itself.[1]

300. In some countries the legislation provides for the setting up of joint bodies within which collective agreements must be, or are normally, concluded. Although often established at the level of a whole branch of activity, some of these bodies are nevertheless also set up at the inter-occupational and plant levels. Usually participation in these joint bodies is restricted to the most representative unions of the branch. It sometimes happens, however, that the conditions laid down by the legislation for participating in the bargaining process could prevent a trade union which is the most representative in its branch of activity from being associated in the collective bargaining procedures.[2] On this point, the Committee is of the opinion that the criteria established by the law should enable such organisations to bargain collectively.

301. Finally, there are several countries[3] in which the legislator has set up specialised institutions[4] whose purpose is to help promote collective bargaining by, for example, studying general problems, drawing up codes of good conduct and giving advice to the parties to help them solve particular problems they may encounter.[5]

----

[1] For example, Benin, United Republic of Cameroon, Central African Republic, Chad, Colombia, Guinea, Ivory Coast, Madagascar, Niger, Nigeria, Peru, Senegal, Tunisia, Venezuela, Zaire.

[2] Belgium, Law of 5 December 1968 and Law of 19 December 1974; see in this connection ILO, 197th Report of the Committee on Freedom of Association, Case No. 918; 208th Report, Case No. 981.

[3] For example in Argentina, Belgium, Luxembourg and Sierra Leone. In Zambia there are standing bodies whose establishment is provided for by law. In the United Kingdom there are permanent bodies established on a voluntary basis. In Benin, Central African Republic, Chad, France, Gabon, Guinea, Ivory Coast, Mali, Morocco, Senegal, Togo and Tunisia there are ad hoc bodies convened with a view to negotiating collective agreements which can be extended.

[4] For example, Canada (the tripartite Canada Labour Relations Board, established in 1975); New Zealand (Industrial Relations Council, established in 1973); Northern Ireland (Labour Relations Agency, created in 1976); United Kingdom (Advisory Conciliation and Arbitration Service, created in 1975).

[5] Besides these specialised institutions numerous other bodies which have not been set up specifically to encourage collective bargaining help to implement activities aimed at promoting collective bargaining (labour inspectorate, advisory bodies such as economic and social committees, national labour councils, national labour relations boards, etc.).

These institutions are entrusted with the specific task (sometimes the sole task) of promoting collective bargaining.

302. Certain rules and practices can facilitate negotiations and help to promote collective bargaining; this is the case, for example, with procedural rules designed to prohibit certain practices which hamper negotiations, such as unfair labour practices.[1] Arrangements can also be made to facilitate the parties', particularly the workers', access to certain information concerning, for example, the economic position of their bargaining unit, wages and working conditions in certain closely related units, or the general economic situation, etc. Some legal systems define precisely the information to be provided.[2]

Voluntary bargaining - autonomy of the parties

303. The principle of voluntary negotiation of collective agreements, and thus the autonomy of the bargaining partners, is a fundamental aspect of Convention No. 98.

304. While machinery and procedures are established in many countries by legislation, they must be designed to facilitate bargaining between the two sides of industry and leave them free to reach their own settlements.

305. There is evidence, however, that more and more countries are imposing restrictions on this freedom either by excluding certain matters from the scope of bargaining or by making the agreement or some of its terms subject to prior agreement or approval by the administrative authorities or the industrial courts.

306. In some countries the range of negotiable questions depends, in part at least, on certain legislative or statutory provisions; these sometimes specify particular questions which the parties have to discuss so as to ensure that they reach their own settlements on the major problems affecting them;[3] others, on the contrary, prohibit the discussion of certain matters for reasons of

----

[1] See above para. 296.

[2] For example, Antigua and Barbuda (Labour Code, 1976); Jamaica (Industrial Relations Code, 1976); Fiji (Industrial Relations Code of Practice, 1973); Sweden (Act respecting co-determination at work, 1976); United Kingdom (Employment Protection Acts, 1975 and 1978, Employment Acts, 1980 and 1982); Denmark, Italy (collective agreements); United States (case law of the National Labor Relations Board). Some other legal systems provide for the communication of certain information to works committees (Austria, Belgium, Finland, France, Federal Republic of Germany, Netherlands, Norway, Zambia).

[3] For example, Mexico (the Federal Labour Law provides that every collective agreement must deal, inter alia, with hours of work, rest days, leave and wages); Philippines (the regulations issued under the Labour Code provide that agreements may not be registered if they do not contain clauses covering family planning, workers' education, reduction in the monotony of work, etc.); USSR (provisions relating to hours of work, rest, industrial safety, fulfilment of production plans, etc.).

general interest or public policy[1] or determine what is or is not a management prerogative.

307. Thus, at the plant level, the legislation of some countries provides that collective agreements may not cover the promotion, transfer, dismissal or reinstatement of workers, nor the recruitment of staff, retrenchment, assignment of duties or, more generally, matters affecting the management and operation of a business.[2]

308. More generally, some countries set aside certain matters for the legislative authority to regulate. Thus, in some countries, collective agreements concluded in new undertakings may not, unless approved by the competent minister, contain provisions with regard to terms and conditions of service which are more favourable than those established in the corresponding legislation. This prohibition applies during the undertaking's first years of operation, a period which may be extended by ministerial decision.[3]

309. There are some countries in which, for general economic reasons, the public authorities lay down standards in regard to conditions of employment, hours of work, leave and, in particular, wages. In this respect, governments, in an increasing number of cases, adopt measures to influence wage determination: decided upon frequently by way of concerted action or non-binding tripartite arrangements, these measures nevertheless at times assume the nature of veritable wage controls in the form of provisions restricting the autonomy of the organisations in regard to wage fixing (for example, a ban on the indexation of the highest wages, a general wage freeze, etc.)

310. Furthermore, in many cases collective agreements must be submitted for approval to an administrative or labour authority or an industrial tribunal before they can enter into force[4] and this authority often withholds its approval or suspends the application of

---

[1] Such provisions include, for example, prohibitions in a great many countries of certain union security clauses or discriminatory provisions regarded as being unacceptable (for example: Trinidad and Tobago, United States).

[2] For example, Malaysia (Industrial Relations Act, ss. 13 and 15); Singapore (Industrial Relations Act, s. 17). In regard to the legislation of Singapore, the Committee of Experts has pointed out that it understands that negotiations, discussions and consultations do, in fact, take place on certain aspects of these matters and that the Government accepts this situation. The Committee has asked the Government to consider the development, through tripartite discussion, of voluntary guidelines for collective bargaining on the issues in question, so as to facilitate the attenuation or removal of the existing statutory limitations (RCE, Report III (Part IVA), ILC, 67th Session, 1981, p. 147).

[3] This is the case in Malaysia (Industrial Relations Act, s. 15) and Singapore (Industrial Relations Act, ss. 24 and 25).

[4] For example, Bolivia (Decree No. 05051/1958, s. 1); Chad (Labour Code, ss. 121 and 122); Kenya (Trade Disputes Act, 1971); Lebanon (Decree No. 17386/64); Libyan Arab Jamahiriya (Labour Code, ss. 64, 65 and 67); Nicaragua (Decree No. 530 of 1980); Singapore (Industrial Relations Act); Syrian Arab Republic (Labour Code, ss. 92, 93 and 98); Tanzania (Act respecting permanent labour tribunals, 1967); Tunisia (Labour Code, s. 38); Yemen (Labour Code, ss. 68, 69 and 71).

all or part of an agreement on the grounds that the settlement is harmful to the economy or does not comply with official directives regarding wages or conditions of employment.

311. In the Committee's view, the right to negotiate wages and conditions of employment freely with the employers and their organisations is a fundamental aspect of freedom of association. Trade unions must have the opportunity to exercise this right without being unduly hampered by legal restrictions. The adoption of restrictive measures violates the principle whereby organisations of workers and employers have the right to organise their activity and formulate their programme of action; it is also incompatible with the principle that collective bargaining should be promoted. Hence, the exclusion from bargaining of certain matters relating to conditions of employment, the submission of collective agreements for prior approval before they can be applied, or enabling them to be declared void because they run counter to the government's economic policy, are all incompatible with Article 4 of Convention No. 98. The Committee would point out that a system of official approval is acceptable in so far as the approval can only be refused on grounds of form and where the clauses of a collective agreement do not conform to the minimum standards set out in the labour law.

312. The principle of the autonomy of the collective bargaining partners was generally recognised during the preparatory discussions leading to the adoption by the International Labour Conference of the Collective Bargaining Convention, 1981 (No. 154). It follows from this principle that the public authorities should, as a general rule, refrain from intervening to alter the content of freely concluded collective agreements. Such intervention could only be justified for major economic and social reasons and in the general interest.

313. Generally, the Committee considers that, rather than subject the validity of collective agreements to government approval, steps should be taken to persuade the parties to collective bargaining to have regard voluntarily in their negotiations to major economic and social policy considerations and the general interest invoked by the government. To achieve this, the considerations should be widely discussed by all parties at the national level through a consultative body (for example, a national social policy advisory board, in accordance with the principle laid down in the Consultation (Industrial and National Levels) Recommendation, 1960 (No. 113)).

314. It might also be prescribed that a collective agreement would come into force only a reasonable length of time after being filed with the competent public authority. If this authority considered that the terms of the proposed agreement were manifestly in conflict with the economic policy objectives recognised as being desirable in the general interest, the case could be submitted for advice and recommendation to an appropriate consultative body, on which the workers' and employers' organisations were represented; this body could indicate to the parties the considerations of general interest that might call for further examination by them of the agreement in question, provided always, however, that the final decision on the matter rested with the parties to the agreement.[1]

----

[1] In the case of <u>Spain</u>, the Committee noted with <u>satisfaction</u> in 1981 that the Workers' Statute of 10 March 1980 merely attributes to the labour authority registration functions in respect of collective agreements, thus eliminating the procedure for approval by the authority provided for in Royal Decree No. 3287/1977. This legislation
(Footnote continued on next page)

315. On the question of wage negotiations, the Committee emphasises that where, for compelling reasons of national economic interest, a government considers that it would not be possible for wage rates to be fixed freely by means of collective negotiations,[1] such a restriction should be imposed as an exceptional measure and only to the

----

(Footnote continued from previous page)

has been developed by Royal Decree No. 1040/81. Similarly, in the case of Panama, the Committee noted with satisfaction in 1982 that Act No. 95/1976, which contained provisions conflicting with Article 4 of Convention No. 98, had been repealed by Act No. 8/1981: the repealed Act had unduly prolonged the period of validity of collective agreements beyond the date of their expiry and had prohibited bargaining during the extended period; it had also exempted newly created undertakings from the obligation to conclude collective agreements during the first two years of their operation and had authorised employers to refuse to conclude a collective agreement where the workers' claims might have endangered the profitability of the undertaking, the Minister of Labour alone being competent to evaluate this criterion.

[1] An increasing number of countries appear to be resorting to statutory wage stabilisation policies, for example: Argentina, Bangladesh, Belgium, Brazil, Canada, Egypt, Jamaica, Netherlands, Nicaragua, Pakistan (nationalised insurance companies and banks), Tanzania.

In Zambia, collective agreements must not contain clauses contrary to the law or the Government's prices and incomes policy or the general interest.

In India, the Government's policy in respect of collective bargaining is reflected in the Five-Year Plan for 1980-85 in which it is indicated, inter alia, that the national wages policy should be based on a rational wages system providing, among other things, for wage differentials that can be justified principally by economic criteria. It is in this context that, even though the primacy of collective bargaining is emphasised, certain guidelines have to be laid down.

In the case of Peru, the Committee noted with satisfaction in 1981 that Legislative Decree No. 23070/1980, which had extended the validity of earlier decrees placing restrictions on collective bargaining, particularly in respect of wages, had ceased to have effect.

It noted in 1978 with satisfaction that, in Tunisia, under Decree No. 73-247 of 26 May 1973, collective agreements may contain provisions with respect to wages and related allowances, job classification and the individual classification of workers in each occupational category.

In the case of Singapore, the Committee noted with interest in 1981 the adoption on 3 December 1980 of Act No. 33/198C amending section 46 of the Employment Act. Under the terms of this amendment an employer may, as of 1 July 1980, at his discretion and without having to seek the prior approval of the Minister for Finance, pay to an employee an annual wage supplement in excess of the amounts specified in subsection 5 of section 46 of the Act up to a maximum of three months' wages of that employee.

extent necessary, without exceeding a reasonable period, and it should be accompanied by adequate safeguards to protect workers' living standards.[1,2] Even greater importance must be attached to this principle because, in cases of successive limitations, a situation is often reached in which the suspension of wage negotiations is of long duration and thus contrary to the promotion of voluntary collective bargaining.

* * *

316. Article 4 of Convention No. 98 provides that governments must take measures, where necessary, to promote voluntary negotiation between employers and workers. It thus guarantees the autonomy of the bargaining parties and means that the government must refrain from interfering in such a manner as to restrict such autonomy.

317. Government interference in the collective bargaining procedure results, in particular, from restrictive legislation on collective bargaining matters and the effects of economic policy measures on the autonomy of the parties.

318. In the Committee's opinion it would normally be contrary to the principles of Convention No. 98 to exclude from collective bargaining certain questions - particularly those concerning conditions of employment - or to make a collective agreement subject to prior approval before it can enter into force or to provide for the possibility of it being declared void because it runs counter to the government's economic policy. The Committee considers that, rather than subject the validity of collective agreements to government approval, steps should be taken to persuade the parties to collective bargaining to have regard voluntarily in their negotiations to major economic and social policy considerations and the general interest invoked by the government.

319. As regards wage bargaining, the Committee stresses that if, for compelling reasons of national economic interest, a government considers that the wage rates cannot be fixed freely by means of collective negotiations, such a restriction should be imposed as an exceptional measure and only to the extent necessary, without exceeding a reasonable period, and it should be accompanied by adequate safeguards to protect workers' living standards.
----

[1] In the United States, the Economic Stabilisation Act adopted in 1970 ceased to have effect in April 1974. Since that time there have been no further wage and price controls. Wages are freely fixed; government action in this field is limited to asking the parties to consent voluntarily to wage limits in certain industries.

In Luxembourg, the Act of 24 December 1977 (as amended) provides for agreements on measures aimed at cutting production costs in the interests of safeguarding employment. This law authorises undertakings affected by particularly serious structural or cyclical difficulties, equivalent to a case of force majeure on the economic plane, to conclude, before the agreed date of expiry of the collective labour agreement, collective agreements on the reduction of production costs in the interests of safeguarding employment. Before negotiations are opened, a tripartite co-ordination committee must give an opinion as to the merits of the request.

[2] See also ILO: Committee on Freedom of Association, 207th Report, Cases Nos. 997 and 999, para. 313.

Organisations
of rural workers

CHAPTER XIII

Rural workers' organisations

320. In many developing countries today, agriculture is still the most important economic activity and the one employing the largest number of workers. In the developed countries and in the socialist economies, agriculture, while not generally employing such a high percentage of the economically active population, nevertheless represents a large share of national production.

321. The problems faced by rural populations are due to a number of causes the effects of which are felt differently in different regions and different countries of the world according to the prevailing system, the composition of the population and the degree and possibilities of agricultural development in the region or the country as a whole.

322. In the developing countries, rural workers are usually among the poorest and most underprivileged segments of the population, and improvement of their lot and their integration in development efforts should be one of the chief objectives of economic and social development. It is essential for this purpose that they have strong, independent and representative organisations and that the necessary machinery be established for ensuring that these organisations can contribute effectively to the development process. One of the best ways of bringing about the necessary changes for successful development is to recognise the major role that can be played by rural workers' organisations and to ensure that they are able to operate freely.[1]

ILO standards other than the Convention and Recommendation concerning rural workers' organisations

323. From the very start, the ILO has been concerned with the problems of rural workers, especially their right of association, and the first standards established in this field related to rural workers: as early as 1921, the International Labour Conference adopted the Right of Association (Agriculture) Convention (No. 11);[2] in 1947, it adopted the Right of Association (Non-Metropolitan Territories) Convention (No. 84), in 1948 the Freedom of Association and Protection of the Right to Organise Convention (No. 87), and in 1949 the Right to Organise and Collective Bargaining Convention (No. 98), which cover rural workers (see Chapters I to XII).

----

[1] See in this connection ILO: Organisations of rural workers and their role in economic and social development, Report VI(1), International Labour Conference, 59th Session, 1974.

[2] See in this connection para. 8 above. Convention No. 11 has been ratified by 104 countries.

324. The Plantations Convention, 1958 (No. 110), which is
tantamount to a social charter for plantation workers, deals, in Parts
IX and X, with the right to organise and collective bargaining and
freedom of association of plantation workers. In 1982, the Conference
adopted an optional Protocol to Convention No. 110 which allows the
exclusion from the Convention's scope of agricultural undertakings
covering less than five hectares and employing not more than 10 workers
within a set period during a set year.

325. Various other ILO instruments have mentioned the need to
set up and develop organisations for rural workers and to improve their
conditions of life.   Mention may be made in particular of the Co-
operatives (Developing Countries) Recommendation, 1966 (No. 127), which
applies to all categories of co-operatives, and the Tenants and Sharecroppers Recommendation, 1968 (No. 132). Among the more recent
instruments, the Labour Administration Convention, 1978 (No. 150), aims
at promoting the conditions of work and life of all categories of rural
workers (Article 7).[1]

326. The problems of rural workers' organisations and their role
in economic and social development have been discussed by ILO regional
conferences and committees, often in connection with activities devoted
to rural development in general:

- the Committee on Work on Plantations has adopted various
   resolutions relating to freedom of association and the exercise
   of trade union rights on plantations and conclusions concerning
   problems and practices of collective bargaining on plantations
   and the exercise of trade union rights;[2]

- the Advisory Committee on Rural Development, in the conclusions
   it adopted at its most recent session, stressed the need to
   promote organisations of rural workers.[3]

Convention No. 141 and Recommendation No. 149

327. The Rural Workers' Organisations Convention, 1975 (No.
141), and Recommendation, 1975 (No. 149), recognise the fundamental
principles of freedom of association and the right to organise for
rural workers;[4] these instruments provide that States are to adopt and
carry out a policy of active encouragement to rural workers'
organisations, particularly with a view to eliminating obstacles to
their establishment, their growth and the pursuit of their lawful
activities, as well as such legislative and administrative
discrimination against rural workers' organisations and their members
as may exist.
----

[1] The Labour Administration Convention (No. 150) and Recommendation
(No. 158) were adopted by the International Labour Conference at its
64th Session in 1978.

[2] See, in particular, Resolution No. 67 and Conclusions No. 69
adopted by the ILO Committee on Work on Plantations at its Sixth and
Seventh Sessions (1971 and 1976).

[3] Advisory Committee on Rural Development, Ninth Session, 1979.

[4] These two instruments were adopted by the International Labour
Conference without opposition.

328.   The main purpose of Convention No. 141 and Recommendation No. 149 is to strengthen the role of rural workers' organisations in economic and social development.

329. Convention No. 141, like the Freedom of Association and Protection of the Right to Organise Convention (No. 87), reaffirms the principle of the right of association of rural workers, a right which is already recognised by Convention No. 87, Article 2.   Article 3 of Convention No. 141, moreover, takes up the principles established by Convention No. 87 and by Articles 1 and 2 of Convention No. 98, while its Preamble recalls the terms of existing Conventions and Recommendations, in particular Conventions Nos. 11, 87 and 98.

330. The Convention provides that States ratifying it are to encourage the establishment and growth of rural workers' organisations and their participation in economic and social development and are to eliminate any discrimination that may exist against rural workers or their organisations as well as any obstacles to their establishment and activities. The Convention also provides that steps are to be taken to promote the widest possible understanding of the need to further the development of rural workers' organisations and of the contribution they can make to improving employment opportunities and general condi- tions of work and life in rural areas as well as to increasing the national income and achieving a better distribution thereof.[1]

331. Recommendation No. 149 describes in detail the role that should be played by rural workers' organisations (in particular the representation and defence of rural workers' interests and their participation in development) and recommends a number of means of encouraging the establishment and growth of such organisations, including legislative and administrative measures. The legislative measures aim primarily at eliminating any obstacles to the establishment and growth of rural workers' organisations. The need to observe the international Conventions concerning the right of association and collective bargaining under national legislation applicable to these workers is stressed in particular. The instrument also mentions the need to establish adequate supervisory machinery to ensure the effective implementation of the relevant legislation.   It further recommends that rural workers' organisations should be associated with planning procedures and the operation of institutions responsible for the development of rural areas, and stresses the need to ensure their effective participation in the formulation, implementation and evaluation of agrarian reform programmes.   In addition, it gives a detailed list of the measures that may be taken to inform the various sectors of the population on questions relating to rural workers and their organisations.   Lastly, it provides for measures to ensure the education and training of these workers and the leaders of their organisations, as well as some financial or material assistance for facilitating the establishment and proper operation of such organisations; this assistance should however be supplied in such a way as not to impair their independence or interests.

332. The analysis here will therefore be confined to a study of the specific aspects of national legislation and practice pointing to a differentiation between rural workers' organisations and other organisations and will not deal with the general aspects of freedom of association and the right to organise except in so far as they shed further light on the analysis made in Chapters I to XII of this survey.
----

[1] Regarding the Convention's scope, see paras. 333 to 335 below.

Scope of the Convention

333.   The Convention applies to all types of organisations of rural workers, including organisations not restricted to but representative of rural workers.[1] It is thus applicable both to organisations composed solely of rural workers and to organisations that, while including other workers as well, represent their interests, for example general trade unions to which various categories of workers belong.[2]

334.   Article 2 of the Convention defines the meaning of "rural workers" under the Convention:

> "For the purposes of this Convention, the term 'rural workers' means any person engaged in agriculture, handicrafts or a related occupation in a rural area, whether as a wage earner or, subject to the provisions of paragraph 2 of this Article, as a self-employed person ..."

335.   It is to be noted that the Convention adopts a very broad notion of the "occupations" coming within its scope and that the Convention applies not only to rural workers who are "wage earners" but also, in certain circumstances, to self-employed persons (Article 2(1)); it gives as examples tenants, sharecroppers and small owner-occupiers. This notion is spelled out by the Convention in Article 2(2), stating that it "applies only to those tenants, sharecroppers or small owner-occupiers who derive their main income from agriculture, who work the land themselves, with the help only of their family or with the help of occasional outside labour and who do not (a) permanently employ workers; or (b) employ a substantial number of seasonal workers; or (c) have any land cultivated by sharecroppers or tenants".[3]

----

[1] For its part, Recommendation No. 149 specifies that "the Co-operatives (Developing Countries) Recommendation, 1966 (No. 127), further remains applicable to the organisations of rural workers falling within its scope".

At its Ninth Session (Geneva, 1979), the Advisory Committee on Rural Development recommended that the promotion of rural workers' organisations and co-operatives should be further developed; some members stressed that co-operatives should be considered as a tool to be utilised by rural workers' organisations.

[2] The Committee of Experts also stressed the right of rural workers to organise jointly with industrial workers (see RCE (Report III (Part 4A), ILC, 68th Session, 1982, C.87, p. 112).

[3] In the agricultural sector, besides wage earners, i.e. workers who supply services in exchange for remuneration either wholly in cash or partly in cash and partly in kind, there are numerous self-employed or partly self-employed workers, generally known as farmers (or peasants or "campesinos"): tenants, sharecroppers, small owner-occupiers. All of these non-wage earning workers, who are often engaged in subsistence farming, live in conditions of poverty similar to and sometimes worse than those of wage earners (ILO, 1974, document D.22.1974).

Recognition and exercise of the right to organise

336. The right of association in general is guaranteed by the constitutions of virtually all countries. The exercise of the right is defined and the conditions for its exercise are determined by legislation.

337. As far as wage-earning agricultural workers are concerned, most legislation recognises their right to organise: the labour codes, the labour laws, the laws on trade unions or, more generally, the laws on the right of association or the civil codes recognise the right of association for all wage earners in general, including agricultural workers.[1]

----

[1] For example, Argentina (Act No. 22105/79 and Regulations No. 640/80); Australia (Conciliation and Arbitration Act, 1904: the interests of most rural workers are covered by the Australian Workers' Union, which is a registered union, but its existence does not prevent rural workers from forming other organisations. However, as regards registration, persons seeking the registration of another organisation covering the same industry or industrial pursuits are generally required to demonstrate why their organisation should also be registered in order to participate in the formal industrial relations system); Austria (Right of Association Act, 1951; Agricultural Workers Act, 1948: laws respecting mandatory organisations - chambers of agriculture - and voluntary organisations - Austrian Confederation of Trade Unions and trade unions of agricultural and forestry workers); Bahamas (Industrial Relations Act, 1970); Barbados (Trade Unions Act, 1964); Belgium (texts identical to those applicable to other workers); Bolivia (Agrarian Reform Act, s. 132, agricultural work is excluded from the general labour law); Brazil (Decree No. 5452/1943; Act No. 5889/1973); United Republic of Cameroon (Labour Code, 1974); Central African Republic (Labour Code, 1961. However, in this country, trade union activities have been suspended since 1 September 1981); Chile (Legislative Decree No. 2756/1979); Colombia (Labour Code, ss. 353 and 356); Cuba (Legislative Decree No. 3/1977); Cyprus (Trade Unions Law, 1965; the Government states that rural workers' unions are the second largest in Cyprus); Denmark (Act No. 156/1961); Ecuador (Labour Code, 1978); Egypt (Trade Unions Act No. 35 of 1976, as amended); Ethiopia (Proclamations Nos. 222 and 223 of 1982); Finland (Associations Act, s. 1; the Government states that a collective agreement ensuring freedom of association for farmers has been concluded); Gabon (Labour Code; Act No. 5/1978); Federal Republic of Germany (Associations Act, 1964); Ghana (Industrial Relations Act, 1965); Greece (Act No. 1264/1982; a Legislative Decree on the establishment of agricultural trade unions will be issued shortly); Guatemala (Labour Code, s. 206); Guyana (Trade Unions Act Cap. 98; the Government states that the right of association is guaranteed); Haiti (Labour Code); Iceland (Trade Unions and Industrial Disputes Act No. 80/1938); India (Trade Unions Act, 1926); Ireland (Industrial Relations Act, 1976; Trade Unions Act, 1871-1975); Israel (Societies Act); Italy (Constitution, s. 39); Japan (Trade Union Law, 1949); Luxembourg (Freedom of Association Act, 1936; the Government states that, owing to the very small number of wage-earning rural workers, no organisation representing rural workers alone has been established so far. Rural workers may join the trade union organisations which are most representative at the national level); Madagascar (Labour Code); Malaysia (Trade Unions Act, 1959; Industrial Relations Act, 1967); Malta (Industrial Relations Act, 1976); Mexico (Federal Labour Act, 1970); Morocco (Dahir No. 1-57-119 (1957) on trade unions); Netherlands (Association and Assembly Act); New Zealand

(Footnote continued on next page)

338. In some countries, however, there are still legislative
restrictions on the establishment of rural workers' organisations.
Some legislation, it seems, contains no provision governing the
establishment or existence of trade unions, allowing doubt to subsist
about the effective possibility for rural workers to form trade
unions.[1] Denial of such a right would be contrary to the freedom of
association Conventions, including Convention No. 141.

339. At times, the right to organise is denied to workers on
farms permanently employing less than a given number of persons.[2]

340. Under the legislation of one country, industrial trade
unions are not allowed to carry out any activities on behalf of
agricultural workers (in practice, however, the situation seems to be
changing).[3]

(Footnote continued from previous page)

(Agricultural Workers Act, 1977; Industrial Relations Act, 1973;
Shearers Act, 1962; it should be noted that three associations have
been established under the Agricultural Workers Act, 1977, including
the Farm Workers' Association (which is not registered in accordance
with the Industrial Relations Act, 1973, but incorporated under the
Incorporated Societies Act, 1908): membership of this association is
voluntary. On the other hand, membership of rural workers in one of
the two other associations which are registered under the Industrial
Relations Act, 1973, is compulsory); Nicaragua (Regulation on trade
union associations and Decree No. 790 of 1979); Norway (established
practice); Panama (Labour Code); Papua New Guinea (Industrial
Organisations Act, Chpt. 173); Philippines (Labour Code, 1974);
Portugal (the right to form trade unions is guaranteed by Article 57 of
the Constitution); Senegal (Labour Code, Act No. 61/34); Spain (Royal
Decree No. 19/1977; Acts Nos. 8/1980 and 51/1980); Suriname (Civil
Code, s. 1668); Sweden (Instrument of Government, 1974); Switzerland
(Civil Code, ss. 60-79); Tunisia (Labour Code); United Kingdom (Trade
Unions and Labour Relations Act, 1974, as amended); Guernsey
(Industrial Disputes and Conditions of Employment Law, 1947-1971); Hong
Kong (Trade Unions Ordinance Cap. 332); Uruguay (Act No. 15137/1981 and
Regulation No. 519/1981); Venezuela (Regulations under the Labour Act,
1973); Zambia (Labour Relations Act, 1971).

[1] For example, Bahrain (agricultural and casual workers are
excluded from the scope of the Labour Act, 1976); Rwanda (Articles 19
and 31 of the 1978 Constitution guarantee freedom of association,
Article 31 providing that any worker may defend his rights through
trade union action. However, the Labour Code excludes workers employed
in agriculture from the scope of the Code).

[2] For example, Dominican Republic (the Labour Code does not apply
to agricultural, agro-industrial, livestock raising and forestry
undertakings continuously and permanently employing no more than ten
workers (s. 265)); Honduras (s. 2 of the Labour Code specifies that the
provisions of the Code are binding on all natural persons,
undertakings, businesses and establishments, with the exception of
agricultural and stock-breeding concerns not permanently employing more
than ten workers).

[3] Liberia: s. 4601-A of the Labour Law prohibits industrial trade
unions and workers' organisations from exercising a privilege or
function on behalf of agricultural workers. However, the Committee
noted with interest in 1982 the Government's statement that the workers
on three plantations have formed joint organisations with industrial
                              (Footnote continued on next page)

341. The legislation of certain States or provinces that excludes rural workers from the laws on anti-union discrimination and collective bargaining tends to impair the development of occupational organisations in agriculture and any effective action on their part in labour relations.[1]

342. Some governments have indicated that their countries have no legislation covering all or part of the matters dealt with in the Convention.[2]

343. In some countries there are no rural workers' organisations although the legislation seems to allow for their creation.[3]

(Footnote continued from previous page)

workers and that under the Bill for the new Labour Law section 4601-A is to be repealed.

[1] United States: agricultural workers (except those employed in undertakings closely related to agriculture but not actually part of a farm operation) are excluded from the provisions of the National Labor Relations Act. A few states, however, have enacted special legislation on labour relations in agriculture. For example, the State of California has established an Agricultural Labour Relations Board which conducts elections to determine collective bargaining representatives and examines complaints of unfair labour practices.

Canada (Ontario and Alberta): the Labour Relations Act does not cover agricultural workers. The Government states that this exclusion is due to the fact that such workers are not recognised as negotiating agents, but this does not prevent them from forming associations to promote the interests of rural workers.

[2] Bangladesh: according to the Government, there are no legislative, administrative or other provisions concerning the matters dealt with in the Convention and no provision for regulating labour relations in the rural sector. It should be noted, however, that the Government has elsewhere indicated (see the General Report of the Committee on Work on Plantations, Eighth Session, 1982) that the Industrial Relations Ordinance, as amended in 1980, applies to plantations and that plantation workers, like other workers, enjoy the legal right to organise trade unions of their own choosing.

Comoros: apart from provisions relating to agricultural work, there are no legislative provisions covering the questions dealt with in the Convention.

The Government of El Salvador states that a legislative decree covering unionism in rural areas is now being studied.

[3] Kuwait: the Government states that there are no agricultural organisations of the kind provided for in the Convention.

Pakistan: the Government states that a tendency to combine is lacking.

Togo: the Government states that trade union organisations for rural workers do not exist at present; however, the 1978 inter-occupational agreement was extended in 1981 to handicraft undertakings employing more than five persons and to agricultural and forestry undertakings.

(Footnote continued on next page)

344. Under the legislation of some States, the members of collective farms, co-operative farms and co-operatives are excluded from the scope of the general labour law.[1] In some of these countries, however, according to information supplied by the governments, organisations have been set up.[2]

345. On the other hand, in other countries, such agricultural workers as members of agricultural co-operatives are not able to join an organisation which is part of the trade union structure.[3]

(Footnote continued from previous page)

Upper Volta: the Government states that under national legislation rural workers enjoy the right to organise but there are no rural workers' organisations in the country.

[1] For example: Angola, Byelorussian SSR, Czechoslovakia, German Democratic Republic, Hungary, Mongolia, Ukrainian SSR, USSR.

[2] The Government of Bulgaria, for example, states that in practice, as a result of the will freely expressed by 955,322 rural workers on 31 December 1981 (including rural co-operative members), these workers joined the Trade Union of Rural Economy and Food Industry Workers.

In Hungary, according to the Government, rural workers do not have a trade union but, in the absence of legislation to the contrary, have the right to form one. The interests of members of co-operative farms are defended by the National Council of Co-operative Farms.

As regards Mongolia, the Committee of Experts noted that agricultural trade union organisations represent the interests of their members - manual workers, employees, farmers and livestock raisers - whether they are members of the agricultural co-operative or not (RCE, 1981).

The Government of the USSR stated, in its 1981 report, that the activities of the trade union organisations of members of collective farms were continuing, and that at present 97.2 per cent of the members of these farms were affiliated to a trade union. In addition, the Government reported a decision taken in August 1977 by the Presidium of the Central Council of Trade Unions concerning the methods of applying the Regulations on the Rights of Factory, Works or Local Trade Union Committees to trade union committees of kolkhozes and of fishermen's kolkhozes. These methods of application were the subject of an agreement between the Union Council of Kolkhoz Members, the Ministry of Agriculture and other ministries concerned. In accordance with this decision, the kolkhoz trade union committee represents the interests of the kolkhoz members as well as those of workers and employees working on the kolkhoz. This trade union committee has legal personality (RCE, 1981).

The situation is similar in the Byelorussian SSR and the Ukrainian SSR.

[3] For example, the Government of Czechoslovakia states that, under the statutes of the Revolutionary Trade Union Movement, members of co-operatives may not become members of the Movement. Co-operative members have not set up any trade union and are organised in the Union of Co-operators.

The Government of the German Democratic Republic states that the members of agricultural co-operatives belong to the Rural Mutualist
(Footnote continued on next page)

346. The Committee considers that such persons should be able to establish, if they so wish, trade union organisations able to promote and defend their interests.

347. As regards self-employed persons within the meaning of the Convention, the legal basis of their right of association may be found in constitutional law or in specific legislation covering particular categories of organisations, in the civil code or in legislation governing the right of association in general. Organisations of rural workers who are self-employed within the meaning of the Convention take different forms, including, inter alia, trade unions, producer associations, farmers' associations, co-operatives, etc.

348. The legislative provisions of many countries provide explicit legal bases for the establishment of one or more of these forms of organisation.[1] In other countries, organisations may be established under the legislation on the right of association.[2]

(Footnote continued from previous page)

Union and that co-operative workers have joined the Trade Union of Agricultural, Food Industry and Forestry Workers.

The Government of Romania states that rural co-operators organised in agricultural co-operatives are covered in particular by the Agricultural Co-operatives Statute; farmers owning private farms are organised in associations and small craftsmen under a handicrafts co-operative system. Manual workers and other persons hired on the basis of an employment contract are covered by the Labour Code.

[1] For example, Algeria, Austria, Barbados, Burundi, Cuba, Cyprus, Ecuador, Ethiopia, Greece, Haiti, India, Ireland, Israel, Japan, Malaysia, Mexico, Nicaragua, Panama, Philippines, Portugal, Spain, Suriname, Tunisia, United Kingdom - non-metropolitan territory of Hong Kong, Zambia.

[2] For example, Belgium, Denmark, Finland (roughly 76 per cent of small farmers are affiliated to the Confederation of Agricultural Producers (CUAP) and there is a similar organisation (SLC) for Swedish-speaking farmers), Federal Republic of Germany, Italy, Luxembourg, Norway, Papua New Guinea, Portugal, Sweden, Switzerland, United Kingdom.

Other legislative provisions mentioned in certain reports: Argentina (Civil Code, s. 33); Colombia (Labour Code, s. 353); Dominican Republic (Act No. 520/1920 respecting non-profiting-making associations; the Government's report seems to indicate, however, that there are also co-operatives in this country).

Australia: although an organisation registered under the Conciliation and Arbitration Act may, in certain limited circumstances, include persons who are not wage earners, it must remain representative of wage earners, otherwise its registration may be withdrawn. As a result, according to the Government, an organisation composed of wage earners and self-employed persons in which self-employed persons are the majority may not obtain registration, even though it is composed of rural workers within the meaning of Article 2 of Convention No. 141.

New Zealand: the Government states that owner-occupiers are not covered by either the Industrial Relations Act (1973) or the Agricultural Workers Act (1977). These persons, like tenants and shareholders, tend to join the Federated Farmers (an employers'
(Footnote continued on next page)

349. The governments of some countries state that existing
legislation does not apply to tenants, shareholders and small owner-
occupiers,[1] that the provisions relating to labourers employed in
agriculture are not applicable to exclusively family undertakings[2] or
that the Convention is regarded as too broad to come within the scope
of national legislation.[3] Other governments, without referring to
specific legislation, report that a certain form of organisation for
these rural workers exists.[4] In other countries, there is apparently no
legislation covering independent rural workers.[5]

350. While recalling that rural workers, as defined by Article
2 of the Convention, have the right to establish organisations, the
Committee considers that the existence of co-operatives or other types
of associations should not prevent rural workers, whether wage earners
or not, from setting up trade unions as the most advanced form of
----
(Footnote continued from previous page)

organisation).

Syrian Arab Republic: according to a statement by the Government,
agricultural workers have the right to join trade unions, whether they
are members of a co-operative or not, under the Rural Organisation Act
(No. 21). The Committee has requested the Government to supply
information on the nature and role of rural co-operative associations
that can be set up by agricultural workers, by farmers working the land
with the help only of members of their family and by landowners whose
holdings do not exceed a prescribed area (RCE, 1982).

[1] Madagascar.

[2] Haiti.

[3] For example, Uruguay: rural workers, however, enjoy the general
right of association under Article 39 of the Constitution (information
supplied by the Government).

[4] For example, Gabon (these are organised workers, like those in
other sectors of the economy), Guyana, Togo (some rural workers belong
to co-operatives; several such associations exist).

The Government of Ghana states that the General Agricultural
Workers' Union has been encouraged to extend its scope of activity to
include other, non-organised agricultural workers.

[5] For example, Bangladesh: the Government states that most rural
workers are self-employed or sharecroppers. The labour legislation
apparently does not apply to these persons.

Pakistan: the Government states that the land is extremely
divided up in rural areas, where there is a majority of small owners
who farm the land for themselves with the help of members of their
family. Accordingly, their problems are different from those of
tenants, sharecroppers or small land occupiers.

The Committee recalls that the scope of Convention No. 141 does
in fact cover these small owner-occupiers (Article 2(1) and (2)); see,
in this respect, para. 333 to 335 above.

Senegal: co-operative associations appear to exist, though the
Government does not specify whether they are for rural workers.

organisation and the one best able to create the necessary conditions for true development in rural areas, particularly in the most underprivileged areas.[1]

351.   The Committee also stresses that, whatever form they may take, rural workers' organisations should be established in ccnfcrmity with Articles 3, 4 and 5 of the Convention: the principles of freedom of association should be wholly observed; the organisaticns should be independent and established on a voluntary basis and should not be subject to any interference, coercion or repression. Governments may play an active part in the establishment and strengthening of rural workers' organisations (e.g. by encouraging their creation, fcstering a propitious climate through legislation, the granting of subsidies and other administrative measures, the training of rural leaders, etc.),[2] but at the same time the policy adopted must ensure that the principles of freedom of association are observed. Steps should also be taken to see that their organisations are not dominated by the privileged or semi-privileged sector of rural society or used for the purpose of exploiting still further the poorest members of the rural population. States should adopt a policy of active encouragement of such organisations, particularly with a view to eliminating obstacles to their establishment, their growth and the pursuit of their lawful activities; rural workers, like all other workers, should enjoy the right to strike as one of the essential means available tc wcrkers and their organisations for furthering and defending their economic and social interests; provisions depriving rural workers of this right are contrary to the freedom of association Conventions including Convention No. 141.[3]

Practical obstacles to the organisation of rural workers

352.   Although legal obstacles to the establishment of rural workers' organisations continue to exist in some countries, while tending to diminish in others, the difficulties facing rural workers in setting up and promoting organisations are often more practical than

----

[1] In some countries, non-wage earning agricultural workers have set up trade unions jointly with wage-earning agricultural workers: for example, Colombia (FANAL), Ecuador (FENOC), Mexico (CNC), Philippines (Federation of Free Farmers (FFF)), Venezuela (Federation of Rural Workers).

[2] See paras. 354 to 363 below.

[3] Such provisions exist, for example, in Costa Rica: s. 369(b) of the Labour Code defines "public services" where strikes are not permitted as "work performed by employees engaged in the sowing, cultivation, care or harvesting of agricultural or silvicultural products or in stockraising, and likewise in the processing of products in cases where they would deteriorate if not immediately treated".

In New Zealand, the provisions governing strikes in the Ccmmerce Act and the Industrial Relations Act relating to essential services are applicable (see para. 213 above).

In the Syrian Arab Republic strikes are prohibited under the Agricultural Labour Code (s. 160) and under s. 19 of the Economic Penal Code.

legal in nature, and relate to the actual exercise of the right of association: the still widespread illiteracy in rural areas, the scattered and isolated nature of agricultural undertakings, the ignorance in which rural populations live as regards their rights, the excessive instability and mobility of seasonal labour, traditional conflicts or antagonisms between various groups who are nevertheless equally underprivileged and poor, difficulties in paying regularly the contributions needed for the establishment and survival of agricultural trade unions and associations, the lack of trade union leaders able to help workers to unite. In this regard, more active assistance from the existing trade union movement would no doubt enhance the possibilities for the promotion of workers' organisations in this sector. The situation is even more complex in the case of migrant and seasonal workers whose instability, mobility and weak position on the labour market make it even more difficult for them than for other workers to exercise their right of association.

353. It should be noted that in practice the most successful attempts of workers to organise have occurred in the plantations sector. The concentration of labour and the existence of processing plants link this sector to the industrial sector and facilitate trade union organisation. Even in this sector, however, obstacles are found to the establishment of trade unions and their activities: the often paternalistic nature of plantation organisation, the fact that the workers are housed on the plantations themselves and the isolation of each plantation have served amongst others as pretexts for certain employers, invoking the principles of the right of property, to forbid trade union leaders access to the plantation, to refuse to supply premises for trade union meetings and to harass those who try to develop a spirit of trade union association among plantation workers on the ground that they are carrying out subversive activities. In examining complaints on these questions, the Committee on Freedom of Association, while fully recognising that plantations are private property, has taken the view that, "as the workers not only work but also live on the plantations, it is only by entering the plantations that trade union officials can normally carry on any trade union activities among the workers and that it is especially important that the entry of such officials to the plantations for the purpose of lawful trade union activities should be readily permitted, provided that there is no interference with the carrying on of the work during working hours and subject to any appropriate precautions for the protection of the estate". In this connection, the Committee on Freedom of Association has drawn attention to the resolution adopted by the Committee on Work on Plantations at its first session in 1950, providing that employers should remove any hindrances in the way of the organisation by plantation workers of free, independent and democratically controlled trade unions and should provide such unions with facilities for the conduct of their normal activities, including free office accommodation, freedom to hold meetings and freedom of entry.[1]

----

[1] See, for example, ILO: Committee on Freedom of Association, 119th Report, Case No. 611, para. 93.

As regards Costa Rica, the Committee of Experts has stressed for many years the need to adopt provisions safeguarding the right of entry to plantations by trade union representatives and the right of plantation workers to hold trade union meetings on the spot.

Promotion of rural workers' organisations

354. Convention No. 141 and Recommendation No. 149 invite governments to facilitate the establishment and growth of rural workers' organisations through a policy of active encouragement to eliminate obstacles. They should also take measures to promote the widest possible understanding of the need to develop such organisations.

355. Many countries actively pursue such a policy,[1] and some have been doing so for many years,[2] often within the framework of an agrarian reform policy.[3] New bodies have been set up to co-ordinate the establishment of renovated structures. The basic task of some is to promote rural workers' organisations. In India, for example, according to the Government the Ministry of Labour set up in 1978 a tripartite Central Standing Committee on Rural Unorganised Labour to advise the Government on the administrative and legislative measures for improving the socio-economic conditions of rural unorganised labour and for the promotion of their organisation. In agreement with the Subcommittee for Rural Workers' Organisations and Education, a scheme to organise rural workers has been drawn up under the sixth Five-Year Plan 1980-85. Framework legislation for agricultural workers is now being studied. Furthermore, the Indian National Rural Labour Federation has published guidelines for rural workers' organisations, stressing the trade union objectives to be pursued, in particular the goals of creating a spirit of organisation and self-reliance and bringing benefits of collective bargaining to all workers. The State of Kerala has enacted specific legislation concerning rural workers (the Agricultural Workers Act. 1974).

356. The Government of the Philippines states that it is pursuing an active policy to develop rural workers' organisations. For this purpose, it has set up the Bureau of Rural Workers (BRW) (Presidential Decrees Nos. 1365 and 1367; Letter of Instruction No. 1209 and Executive Order No. 779). The Bureau's principal objective, which is to protect and promote the welfare of rural workers so that they may participate fully in national development, requires a direct approach, focused on rural workers as the object of development. To achieve its targets, the Bureau is carrying out four programmes aimed at organising rural workers: (1) an education and organisation programme, inter alia, to encourage, develop and promote the establishment and growth of rural workers' organisations; (2) a rural project development programme, in which priority is given to the organised labour sector over the unorganised sector in order to strengthen existing organisations and encourage other rural workers to organise; (3) a social amelioration programme; and (4) a research programme. The Bureau not only provides assistance to specially defined rural organisations but has extended its operations to include organisations of ambulant, intermittent and itinerant workers, those self-employed in both urban and rural areas and those without a definite or fixed employer, as well as underemployed workers.

----

[1] For example, Algeria, Cape Verde, Colombia, Cuba, Cyprus, Ecuador, India, Mexico, Nicaragua, Philippines, Portugal.

[2] For example, Japan (Law No. 127/1961; this law provides that the State is to take the necessary measures for organisational improvement of organisations related to agriculture).

[3] For example, Cape Verde, Colombia, Cuba, India, Mexico, Portugal, Suriname.

357. Other bodies or ministries also take an active part in promoting the status of rural workers.[1] Rural workers' organisations are sometimes represented here.

358. Some governments have supplied information about the participation of rural workers in the economic and social effort, particularly in the rural development programmes and national planning. In Cuba, for example, Act No. 1322/1976 aims at promoting the active participation of workers in the preparation, supervision and implementation of the plans.

359. In Ecuador, priority in the National Development Plan for 1980-84 is given to an over-all rural development policy designed for the benefit of small landowners, agricultural wage earners, landless peasants and the marginal rural population. The beneficiaries take an active part in the design, implementation and co-ordination of the Plan.   In Nicaragua, the representatives of rural organisations participate, in particular, in the national and regional agrarian reform councils and in production councils.

360. In many countries, seminars, lectures, courses and educational programmes for rural workers are carried out to activate their interest in promoting organisations able to represent them, negotiate on their behalf, participate in programmes consistent with their interests and provide training services to their members.[2] Some

----

[1] For example, Argentina (National Board for Rural Labour (tripartite); Act No. 22248/1980), Colombia (Colombian Institute of Agrarian Reform); Cuba (Planning, Fertile Lands and Food Council, Act respecting central state administration No. 1322/1976); Cyprus (agricultural and economic advisory committees (tripartite)); Dominican Republic (Agricultural Insitute); Finland (Board of Labour Protection); Jamaica (Social Development Commission); Mexico (Ministry of Agrarian Reform and various tripartite advisory committees concerning workers in general); Portugal (Department of Agricultural Extension, Decree No. 221/77); Senegal (National Advisory Board, which includes a representative of agricultural trade unions); Spain (Rural Development Agency); Sweden (National Board of Agriculture); Tunisia (Rural Development Board).

[2] For example, Algeria (efforts have been made towards the development of rural animation centres concerning child-rearing and home economy; the training of engineers and technicians).

Argentina (Act No. 22248 is intended, in particular, to formulate a national policy for the intensive technical training of rural workers).

Colombia (Simon Bolivar literacy campaign, theoretical and practical courses on rural life and labour law).

Cuba (numerous modern guidance centres, literacy campaigns).

Cyprus (rural workers' organisations collaborate in particular with the Ministry of Agriculture regarding educational and training measures).

Ecuador (seminars, courses, lectures on the organisation of handicraft workers, rural literacy plan).

Haiti (co-operative training course for technicians assigned to
(Footnote continued on next page)

countries broadcast educational and training programmes both for rural workers and for making the population at large alive to their problems, particularly radio and television programmes.[1]

361. Some governments have supplied information on available credit facilities,[2] efforts made in the field of housing[3] and
----
(Footnote continued from previous page)

development programmes, especially in rural, semi-rural and suburban areas) (Act No. 14/1953 and Decree of 31 March 1981).

India (educational programmes of the National Labour Institute, the Indian Institute of Public Administration, the National Institute of Rural Development and the Central Board for Workers' Education. One of the purposes of the Central Board, a tripartite body, is to develop strong and more effective trade unions). The Government considers that the reforms made (agrarian reforms, minimum wage, etc.) are partly due to the educational effort; the Five-Year Plan provides for adequate measures for the benefit of women in rural areas.

Jamaica (community centres and social programmes to promote development of leaders and training in co-operatives).

Mexico (education and vocational training for members of various associative organisations in rural areas; in particular, the Co-operative Act and the Agrarian Reform Act, sections 148, 149 and 184; services of the CENAPRO and the ARMO).

Nicaragua (literacy campaigns; education programmes organised by PROCAMPO; technical training programmes).

Pakistan (mass education in rural areas).

Philippines (the education and organisation programme of the BRW comprises two aspects: (a) assistance and encouragement towards organisation and (b) organisational strengthening. It includes educational courses, seminars for leaders and vocational training).

Portugal (Act No. 3/1979, Decree No. 221/1977).

Efforts in this field are also being made in other countries, including Finland, Japan, Luxembourg, Mongolia, Sweden, Tanzania, Ukrainian SSR and the United States (Act CETA-291/SC, para. 873).

In New Zealand, there are two universities specialised in agriculture and a rural training council.

[1] For example: Austria, Colombia, Cuba, Finland, India, Japan, Mexico, New Zealand, Norway, Philippines, Portugal, Sweden, Switzerland.

[2] For example: Algeria, Colombia (credits granted to organisations may not be made subject to conditions involving any restriction on the freedom of the organisations or their members), Cyprus, Guatemala, Haiti (handicraft credit service), Malaysia, Mexico, New Zealand, Papua New Guinea, Tunisia.

[3] Argentina (Act No. 22248/80 lays down the minimum conditions for food and housing facilities for non-permanent workers), Cuba, New Zealand (Agricultural Workers Act, 1977, s. 49).

occupational safety and health[1] cr, generally, the conditions of work and life of rural workers.[2]

362. Other governments have supplied information on collective bargaining procedures.[3] Article 5 of Recommendation No. 149 provides that rural workers' organisations "should, as appropriate, be able to (a) represent, further and defend the interests of rural workers, for instance by undertaking negotiations and consultations at all levels on behalf of such workers collectively ...".

363. As regards the authorities responsible for supervising the application of legislation or regulations, the information supplied by governments indicates that in the great majority of cases this responsibility rests with the Ministry of Labour, and the labour inspectorate in particular,[4] although other ministries or bodies may also be assigned the task.[5] One government states that no arrangements exist for labour administration and labour inspection in rural areas.[6]

----

[1] For example, Canada (Province of Quebec: the Industrial Accidents Act applies to the agricultural sector), Cuba (rural workers are covered by Acts Nos. 3/1977 and 24/1979 on occupational safety and health and social security), Ecuador (Decree No. 724/1980 and Act No. 81/1981), Mexico (Federal Labour Act, s. 472), New Zealand (Agricultural Workers' Act of 1977, s. 56), United States (migrant health centres programme - MHCT).

[2] Byelorussian SSR, German Democratic Republic, Romania, Ukrainian SSR, USSR (Order of the Council of Ministers, 1982, on the implementation of the food programme).

[3] For example, Cyprus, Finland, Federal Republic of Germany, Japan, Netherlands, New Zealand, Norway, Portugal (Decree No. 519-C1/1979, government directives of 1979 and 1981; collective agreements were concluded between the Ribatejo and the Alentejo farmers and the Federation of Agricultural Workers in 1980 and 1981, respectively).

[4] For example, Australia (at the level of the various states; at the federal level: Industrial Relations Bureau), Brazil, United Republic of Cameroon, Colombia, Djibouti, Dominican Republic, Egypt, Gabon, Guatemala, Haiti, Jamaica, Liberia, Luxembourg, Madagascar, Malaysia, Malta, Morocco, New Zealand, Nicaragua (as well as the Ministry of Agrarian Reform), Portugal, Spain, Togo, Uruguay, Venezuela.

[5] For example, Burundi (Ministry of Rural Development), Cuba (National Committee of Labour and Ministry of Agriculture), Cyprus (Ministries of the Interior and Industry), Ecuador (Ministry of Agriculture, Ministry of Social Welfare), Finland (Ministry of Social Affairs and Health), Israel (Ministry of Agriculture and various commissions), Japan (Ministry of Agriculture, Forestry and Fishery, local authorities), Mexico (Ministry of Agrarian Reform, Ministries of Labour, Agriculture, Commerce and Education), Pakistan (National Industrial Relations Commission), Zimbabwe (a ministry recently established).

[6] Bangladesh: the Government also states that it is not planned to adopt measures to give effect to the Convention in the near future.

*
*   *

364. Rural workers within the meaning of the Convention[1] have the right to establish organisations that are independent and voluntary in character and free from all interference, coercion or repression; States should carry out a policy of active encouragement to rural workers' organisations, particularly with a view to eliminating obstacles to their establishment, their growth and the pursuit of their lawful activities as well as any legislative and administrative discrimination that may exist against such organisaticns. The existence of co-operatives or other forms of association should not prevent rural workers, whether wage earners or not, from establishing trade union organisations. Rural workers should, in their activities, enjoy the right to strike in order to defend their economic and social interests.

365. The obstacles facing rural workers in establishing organisations are often as practical as they are legal in character. Convention No. 141 provides that steps are to be taken to promote the widest possible understanding of the need to further the development of rural workers' organisations and Recommendation No. 149 advocates a number of means that may facilitate the establishment and growth of such organisations. This survey shows that the means implemented vary considerably from one country to another, some having established or planning to establish a systematic policy on the matter, while others tend to resort rather to ad hoc measures.

----

[1] For the scope of the Convention, see paras. 333 to 335 above.

**Difficulties and ratification prospects
and final remarks**

CHAPTER XIV

Ratification of Conventions:
difficulties and prospects

366. A number of governments have mentioned the reasons which prevent them, temporarily at least, from ratifying one or more of the freedom of association Conventions; others have stated that they intend to ratify some of them.

Convention No. 87

Difficulties

367. Some governments state in general terms that there are difficulties as regards the application or ratification of the Convention[1], or point out that their legislation is the most suitable for their economic and social systems[2] or is necessary for the healthy development of the trade union movement and harmonious industrial relations.[3]

368. Others point to specific difficulties connected with particular aspects of the Convention: the Government of Brazil mentions difficulties linked, for example, to Articles 2 and 4 of the Convention; the Government of El Salvador states that Article 9 of the Convention is not applicable under national law since the armed forces and the police are governed by special texts. The Committee of Experts has already drawn the attention of the Government of El Salvador, in its General Survey of 1973, to the fact that according to Article 9 the extent to which the guarantees provided for in the Convention apply to the armed forces and the police is to be determined by national law and regulations. Consequently, States ratifying the Convention can decide on the extent to which the persons in question shall enjoy the right to organise.

369. The Government of India states that the Central Civil Services (Recognition of Associations) Rules, 1959, and the Central Civil Services (Conduct) Rules, 1964, are not fully in line with the Convention.

370. The Government of Malaysia points out that trade unions are formed on the basis of the same trades, occupations or economic branches and that workers may join only the union which represents their own trade, occupation or branch. The Government considers the legislation to be adequate in the national context.

----

[1] For example, Bahamas, Saudi Arabia, Indonesia, Sri Lanka.

[2] Chile.

[3] Singapore.

371. The Government of Morocco points out that under national legislation persons responsible, in any capacity whatsoever, for the administration or running of a trade union must be of Moroccan nationality. This provision prevents the ratification of the Convention for the time being.

372. The Government of New Zealand refers to a series of legislative provisions which, it considers, are incompatible with the Convention and prevent its ratification: certain legal restrictions on the recognition of trade unions, preference clauses, the Fishing Industry (Union Coverage) Act, which explicitly prevents workers from joining an organisation of their own choosing, restrictions on strikes, and the Minister's power to deregister a union.

373. The Government of Turkey refers to the proclaiming of martial law in 1980 and in particular to the suspension of certain organisations and restrictions on their activities; it states that when this temporary period has expired organisations will be able to carry on their activities freely (it does not state its intentions regarding the ratification of the Convention).

374. The Government of Zambia refers to a series of provisions which, it considers, are incompatible with the Convention, preventing its early ratification: trade union monopoly, compulsory affiliation of workers' and employers' organisations to the two central organisations; a denial of registration to trade unions if the category of workers concerned are eligible for membership of an already existing registered trade union; prohibition of affiliation of trade unions to international organisations without prior approval from the authorities; control of funds and denial of the right of organisations to accept assistance in any form from any source outside the country without approval from the Minister. The Government nevertheless states that the Industrial Relations Act, 1971, is continually monitored and open to consultations between workers and employers and the Government with a view, inter alia, to adopting measures to give effect to some of the provisions of the Convention. In particular, the Government states that Article 3 is being reviewed with a view to modifying the meaning of "essential services" so that it incorporates only those services whose interruption would endanger the existence or well-being of the whole or part of the population.

375. The Government of Zimbabwe, while pointing to certain difficulties as regards Articles 3 and 4 of the Convention, considers that there are no other major difficulties to prevent or delay ratification of the Convention. However, it also states that domestic service employees and public servants are not covered by the Industrial Conciliation Act.

Ratification prospects

376. The Government of Rwanda states that as far as legislation is concerned there are no major difficulties to prevent ratification of the Convention but that this is being delayed for practical reasons.

377. The Government of Papua New Guinea states that the Industrial Organisations Act guarantees freedom of association.

378. The Government of the United States, in its report, states that the situation has not changed as regards ratification. (It may be recalled that in 1949 the Convention was submitted to the Senate with a request for its advice and consent to ratification.)

379. The Government of Burundi has decided to postpone ratification.

Convention No. 98

Difficulties

380. The Government of Chile states that the legislation in force is the most suitable for the economic and social system.

381. The Governments of El Salvador, Kuwait and Madagascar indicate as a difficulty the fact that the armed forces and the police are not covered by national laws and regulations on trade unions. The Committee of Experts recalls that, as in the case of Convention No. 87, Article 5 of Convention No. 98 specifies that the extent to which the guarantees provided for in the Convention apply to the armed forces and the police is for national laws or regulations to determine. Consequently, States ratifying the Convention decide freely whether and to what extent these persons are to enjoy the right to organise.

382. The Government of India refers to its previous report in which it pointed out that its national laws and regulations contained no provision protecting workers against acts of anti-union discrimination upon recruitment and referred to restrictions on the right of civil servants to organise and bargain collectively.

383. The Government of Switzerland states that generally its reason for not being able to ratify the Convention lies in the fact that present laws and regulations contain no special provision affording workers the protection required by the Convention, at least as regards recruitment. The Government adds that Article 56 of the Federal Constitution guarantees freedom of association, but that this principle is only directly valid as regards the public authorities. However, freedom of coalition or association can be threatened by individuals. This is the case, for example, when the positive freedom of association is endangered by termination of a contract of employment or an employer's refusal to draw up a contract of employment. In accordance with the Swiss constitutional system these matters should be clarified at the legislative level. The Government adds that no action has been taken in this connection recently.

384. The Government of Mexico refers to its previous report in which it stated that its national laws and regulations permitted the inclusion in collective agreements of trade union security clauses; the Committee has already informed the Government that these trade union security clauses are a matter for national practice.

385. The Government of New Zealand considers that the main obstacle to ratification of Convention No. 98 lies in its close relation with Convention No. 87, whose ratification would require a sweeping change in the industrial relations system. The Committee has already stated in its previous General Survey that it would be in no way illogical for a State to ratify Convention No. 98 without having ratified Convention No. 87.[1]

----

[1] See ILO, General Survey, Report III (Part 4B), ILC, 58th Session, 1973, para. 189.

386. As regards Canada, the Committee notes with interest that, according to the Government, the Canadian Labour Code is practically in line with Convention No. 98 and that there is substantial compliance in all provinces with the basic provisions of the Convention. However, the Government mentions laws of certain provinces which exclude certain workers from the legislation respecting labour relations (Prince Edward Island, Nova Scotia, Ontario and Alberta) or which contain provisions that seem to run counter to the principle of voluntary negotiation (Quebec).

387. The Government of Rwanda states that the appropriate machinery has not yet been set up to give practical effect to Articles 1 and 4 of the Convention, but that steps are now being taken that will enable its implementation.

388. The Government of Zimbabwe, while pointing to certain restrictions as regards voluntary collective bargaining, states that there are no major difficulties to prevent or delay ratification of the Convention.

Ratification prospects

389. The Government of the Netherlands states that Article 6 of the Convention has been one of the main obstacles to its ratification. Now that Convention No. 151 has been ratified, the problem can be overcome since the scope of this Convention covers all categories of public servants. The Government adds that the advisability of a legislative provision to apply Article 1 may be considered.

390. The Government of Togo states that a study of the provisions of the Convention is being carried out. The Government of Burundi has decided to postpone ratification; it states, however, that measures are being contemplated to implement the provisions of the Convention.

391. The Government of the United States points out that the situation regarding ratification has not changed.

392. The Government of Zambia states that although there are no major obstacles to ratification, it is not considered advisable to ratify the Convention at the present time.

Remarks of the Committee

393. The Committee of Experts notes with satisfaction that, since 1973, 17 States have ratified Convention No. 87 (Antigua and Barbuda, Australia, Colombia, Comoros, Djibouti, Dominica, German Democratic Republic, Haiti, Portugal, Saint Lucia, Seychelles, Spain, Suriname, Swaziland, Switzerland, Yemen and Venezuela) and that 20 States have ratified Convention No. 98 (Angola, Antigua and Barbuda, Australia, Bahamas, Bolivia, Cape Verde, Colombia, Comoros, Djibouti, Dominica, Fiji, German Democratic Republic, Grenada, Guinea-Bissau, Lebanon, Papua New Guinea, Saint Lucia, Spain, Swaziland and Yemen).[1]

----

[1] Some of these ratifications (Spain, Portugal) came about after a complete revision of the legislation, a fact which the Committee of Experts notes with satisfaction.

394. As regards certain other States, the Committee notes that
some of the difficulties emphasised in the Governments' reports were
already mentioned in 1973 and that consequently the situation would not
appear to have changed. The Committee can only express the hope that
the governments concerned will be able to consider undertaking the
changes in law and in practice that are deemed necessary for ratifying
the two Conventions.

Convention No. 141

Difficulties

395. A large number of reports refer to difficulties that could
delay or prevent ratification of the Convention.

396. Some governments consider that their legislation is not in
harmony with the Convention. For example:

- Australia: although an organisation registered under the
Conciliation and Arbitration Act can, in certain limited circumstances,
include persons who are not employees, it must remain representative of
employees and, if it ceases to be so representative, it is liable to be
deregistered. An organisation whose membership comprises self-employed
persons and employees, in which the majority are self-employed, could
not obtain registration even if it comprised rural workers within the
scope of the definition in Article 2 of the Convention. Articles 4 and
5 also give rise to problems in the Australian context. The Government
also states in its report that the establishment of unions in any one
sector of the economy, such as the rural sector, would not be simply
achieved.

- Bangladesh: there are no legislative, administrative or other
provisions in respect of the matters dealt with in the Convention. The
Government specifies that it has no plans for adopting measures to
implement the Convention in the near future.

- United Republic of Cameroon: the scope of the Convention is too
broad, going beyond the framework of national law and practice in this
field.

- Canada: certain provincial laws exclude some or all agricultural
workers from the scope of the labour standards. The Government
considers that it would be advisable to examine in detail whether the
policies of the provincial governments meet the requirements of the
Convention as regards encouraging organisations of rural workers.

- Ireland: the definition of a rural worker does not correspond to
that given in the Industrial Relations Act. Furthermore, the
Government states, a policy aiming to encourage the creation of
organisations of rural workers could give rise to difficulties since
workers and employers are accustomed to take the steps necessary for
their own development.

- Japan: the Agricultural Co-operative Organisation, the
Prefectural Agricultural Conference and the National Agricultural
Conference are subject to certain restrictions that might be
incompatible with Article 3 of the Convention.

- Madagascar: the texts in force only apply to wage earners.

- New Zealand: substantial differences, as well as the difficulties connected with Convention No. 87, prevent ratification. The Agricultural Workers Act was adopted after the adoption of the Convention by the International Labour Conference and there are no plans for measures to implement the Convention.

- United States: the subject-matter of the Convention has been regarded as appropriate for action primarily by the States. The noted wide variance of coverage by State laws which give effect to all or some of the provisions of the Convention may pose some difficulties in securing ratification.

- Uruguay: the legislation in force (Act No. 15137 and Decree No. 647/978) applies only to wage earners and the Government considers that it is not technically possible to co-ordinate the content of the Convention with national legislation.

397. Other governments, while sometimes making reference to legislative difficulties, refer also to an economic and social context that is unfavourable to the development of organisations of rural workers. For example:

- Burundi: the difficulty lies in the fact that organisations of rural workers are very recent, embryonic, institutions which need to be consolidated.

- Pakistan: customs and traditions cannot be replaced by strict legislative action; the Government lists a series of social, cultural and economic factors which explain why the process of organising rural workers is a slow one.

- Rwanda: at the practical level, material difficulties are delaying the ratification of the Convention.

- Upper Volta: the reasons for postponing ratification of the Convention lie in the social, cultural and economic situation of the rural world in Upper Volta.

- Zimbabwe: the difficulties that might delay ratification are connected with the present stage of economic and social development and the lack of an administrative or legal framework respecting persons engaged in rural handicrafts.

398. One government (Panama) considers that its own legislation is ahead of the Convention; another (Luxembourg) considers that its trade union structure and the pattern of association of self-employed rural workers would not correspond to the requirements of the Convention. Another government (Portugal) considers that it would be difficult to attain the objectives and measures provided for in Articles 4, 5(1) and 6 of the Convention because of the recent structure of the organisations of rural workers and the lack of a global policy based on broad participation.

Ratification prospects

399. The Committee notes with interest that France has begun to take steps towards ratification.

400. It notes that several governments - Colombia, Gabon, Liberia, Morocco and Venezuela - state that there are no difficulties

inherent in the Convention to prevent its ratification. The Government of Argentina sees no difficulties in principle but considers that it would first be appropriate to clarify certain problems with which it is confronted as regards the application of Convention No. 87.

401. The Government of the German Democratic Republic states that there has been no need for any change and that the implementation of the Convention and of the Recommendation has not given rise to any difficulties. The Government of Yugoslavia considers that the Convention and Recommendation are satisfactorily applied. Likewise, the Government of the USSR states that national law and practice call for no change with regards to the provisions of the Convention and the Recommendation.

402. Another country, Mongolia, states that the matter is presently being studied.

403. The Government of Greece, for its part, considers that its legislation complies with the provisions of Convention No. 141 but points to certain difficulties in respect of the Recommendation.

404. A number of countries are not planning to ratify the Convention because of the structure of their economies, which are essentially industrial: Barbados - the concept "rural" does not really apply to Barbados; Kuwait - the agricultural sector plays no part in the economy; Singapore - "urbanised" economy.

405. Three countries, Indonesia, Qatar and Turkey are not contemplating ratification in the near future.

406. Other governments consider that their practice (Czechoslovakia) or their legislation (Chile) are suited to the national framework or the present stage of development (Malaysia).

407. Some governments give no particular information (Belgium, Senegal, Togo).

Remarks of the Committee

408. The Committee notes with satisfaction that 23 States, of which more than half are developing countries,[1] have ratified the Convention since it was adopted in 1975 and notes with interest that France is taking steps with a view to ratification.

409. Without going into a detailed discussion of the difficulties described by the governments, the Committee considers that some of them, in view of the comments set forth in Chapter XIII above, should be able to overcome these difficulties. In this regard the Committee of Experts points out that the ILO is at the disposition of the member States for any advice or assistance required with a view to facilitating the ratification of the Convention.

---

[1] List of States having ratified Convention No. 141, see Appendix III.

CHAPTER XV

Final remarks

410.   Thirty-five years have passed since the General Assembly of the United Nations adopted the Universal Declaration of Human Rights and the International Labour Conference adopted the basic principles and standards in respect of freedom of association which form part of those fundamental human rights that the ILO has solemnly undertaken to promote and in favour of which it has always worked through its standard-setting activities and the jurisprudence of its supervisory bodies.[1]

411.   On these firmly established and universally recognised principles, which define the fundamental guarantees of civil liberties that should constitute the common ideal to be aimed at by all peoples and all nations, depends the enjoyment of the guarantees contained in the freedom of association Conventions. This enjoyment is effective only if the fundamental civil liberties are recognised and safeguarded since the exercise of trade union rights depends not only on formal rules and institutional provisions but also on their practical application.

412.   In undertaking the present study, the Committee has not lost sight of the problems and difficulties facing countries with different political, economic and social backgrounds, and countries whose stages of development differ as regards the application of the Conventions under review. However, the Committee has not departed from the approach it has constantly followed to determine the extent to which Conventions are applied. This approach, which is inherent in its very mandate, consists in examining, from a strictly legal point of view, and regardless of the political, economic and social system or situation, whether countries which have ratified Conventions are actually carrying out the consequent obligations by which they are bound.   In the view of the Committee it is only through the systematic and uniform application of this approach that an objective assessment of the situation can be made and that opinions can be formulated as to the compatibility of national legislation and practice with the principles and standards contained in the Conventions which are the subject of this study.

413.   The Committee has been able to note with satisfaction in the course of this survey that in some countries, following sweeping political changes, fundamental freedoms and trade union rights have been fully recognised or re-established, and that, in other countries, certain improvements in laws and regulations have brought national legislation more into conformity with the principles and standards of the Conventions. The Committee notes, however, with concern that in a

----

[1] See above, Chapter I.

number of other countries the situation has hardly changed or has even
deteriorated and that the law and/or practice do not correspond to the
requirements of the Conventions.

414. This is confirmed by the fact that in recent years the
number of cases brought to the attention of the Governing Body
Committee on Freedom of Association has increased alarmingly. These
cases involve issues of law or of fact and alleged violations of the
principles of freedom of association. The Committee of Experts is
deeply concerned to note that many of these cases concern not only
infringements of some of the most fundamental principles set forth in
the Conventions, but also the violation of fundamental human rights,
respect for which is essential for the free exercise of trade union
rights.

415. Moreover, the Committee must point out that while
Conventions Nos. 87 and 98 are among the most ratified, there are
nevertheless 54 member States which have not ratified Convention No. 87
and 38 which have not ratified Convention No. 98. It is clear that
further ratifications of these instruments would help to strengthen the
action of the ILO for the protection of trade union rights.

416. As regards Convention No. 141 and Recommendation No. 149,
the Committee hopes that the present study will have enabled certain
points of interpretation to have been clarified, thus enabling an
increased number of countries, and in particular developing countries,
to ratify Convention No. 141. This Convention should offer member
States an indispensable means of improving the living conditions of
rural workers who are still among the poorest of the poor and should
enable these workers to become actively involved in their own
development and that of their nation.

417. In carrying out this General Survey, the Committee was able
to see that the promotion of freedom of association was constantly
running into new obstacles. For example, there is a growing tendency
for the ever-increasing economic problems confronting States to create
real difficulties in this respect. Whatever these difficulties, it
must never be forgotten that trade unions have a vital function to
fulfil in society: that of making a decisive contribution to social
justice. It is essential for these organisations to provide a
genuinely free forum for all workers and employers, particularly since
conflicts of interest are likely to continue. While deprival of trade
union rights certainly gives rise to violent situations, all forms of
limitations on individuals' freedom of association may result sooner or
later in alienating people from trade unionism itself, which can only
prove harmful to the interests of the workers and, in the final event,
of the community as a whole.

418. It is important therefore that workers and employers should
be able, through independent organisations free from any outside
interference, to express their aspirations and to provide an
indispensable contribution to economic development and social progress.
In carrying out the present survey, the Committee has tried to work
towards this fundamental ILO objective.

APPENDIX I

TEXT OF THE SUBSTANTIVE PROVISIONS OF CONVENTIONS
NOS. 87, 98 AND 141 AND OF RECOMMENDATION NO. 149

Freedom of Association and Protection of the Right
to Organise Convention, 1948 (No. 87)

Article 1

Each Member of the International Labour Organisation for which
this Convention is in force undertakes to give effect to the following
provisions.

Article 2

Workers and employers, without distinction whatsoever, shall have
the right to establish and, subject only to the rules of the
organisation concerned, to join organisations of their own choosing
without previous authorisation.

Article 3

1.   Workers' and employers' organisations shall have the right
to draw up their constitutions and rules, to elect their
representatives in full freedom, to organise their administration and
activities and to formulate their programmes.

2.   The public authorities shall refrain from any interference
which would restrict this right or impede the lawful exercise thereof.

Article 4

Workers' and employers' organisations shall not be liable to be
dissolved or suspended by administrative authority.

Article 5

Workers' and employers' organisations shall have the right to establish and join federations and confederations and any such organisation, federation or confederation shall have the right to affiliate with international organisations of workers and employers.

Article 6

The provisions of Articles 2, 3 and 4 hereof apply to federations and confederations of workers' and employers' organisations.

Article 7

The acquisition of legal personality by workers' and employers' organisations, federations and confederations shall not be made subject to conditions of such a character as to restrict the application of the provisions of Articles 2, 3 and 4 hereof.

Article 8

1.   In exercising the rights provided for in this Convention workers and employers and their respective organisations, like other persons or organised collectivities, shall respect the law of the land.

2.   The law of the land shall not be such as to impair, nor shall it be so applied as to impair, the guarantees provided for in this Convention.

Article 9

1.   The extent to which the guarantees provided for in this Convention shall apply to the armed forces and the police shall be determined by national laws or regulations.

2.   In accordance with the principle set forth in paragraph 8 of article 19 of the Constitution of the International Labour Organisation the ratification of this Convention by any Member shall not be deemed to affect any existing law, award, custom or agreement in virtue of which members of the armed forces or the police enjoy any right guaranteed by this Convention.

Article 10

In this Convention the term "organisation" means any organisation of workers or of employers for furthering and defending the interests of workers or of employers.

Article 11

Each Member of the International Labour Organisation for which this Convention is in force undertakes to take all necessary and appropriate measures to ensure that workers and employers may exercise freely the right to organise.

Right to Organise and Collective Bargaining Convention, 1949 (No. 98)

Article 1

1.   Workers shall enjoy adequate protection against acts of anti-union discrimination in respect of their employment.

2.   Such protection shall apply more particularly in respect of acts calculated to -

(a)   make the employment of a worker subject to the condition that he shall not join a union or shall relinquish trade union membership;

(b)   cause the dismissal of or otherwise prejudice a worker by reason of union membership or because of participation in union activities outside working hours or, with the consent of the employer, within working hours.

Article 2

1.   Workers' and employers' organisations shall enjoy adequate protection against any acts of interference by each other or each other's agents or members in their establishment, functioning or administration.

2.   In particular, acts which are designed to promote the establishment of workers' organisations under the domination of employers' organisations, or to support workers' organisations by financial or other means, with the object of placing such organisations under the control of employers or employers' organisations, shall be deemed to constitute acts of interference within the meaning of this Article.

Article 3

Machinery appropriate to national conditions shall be established, where necessary, for the purpose of ensuring respect for the right to organise as defined in the preceding Articles.

Article 4

Measures appropriate to national conditions shall be taken, where necessary, to encourage and promote the full development and utilisation of machinery for voluntary negotiation between employers or employers' organisations and workers' organisations, with a view to the regulation of terms and conditions of employment by means of collective agreements.

Article 5

1.   The extent to which the guarantees provided for in this Convention shall apply to the armed forces and the police shall be determined by national laws or regulations.

2.   In accordance with the principle set forth in paragraph 8 of article 19 of the Constitution of the International Labour Organisation the ratification of this Convention by any Member shall not be deemed to affect any existing law, award, custom or agreement in virtue of which members of the armed forces or the police enjoy any right guaranteed by this Convention.

Article 6

This Convention does not deal with the position of public servants engaged in the administration of the State, nor shall it be construed as prejudicing their rights or status in any way.

Rural Workers' Organisations Convention, 1975 (No. 141)

Article 1

This Convention applies to all types of organisations of rural workers, including organisations not restricted to but representative of rural workers.

Article 2

1.   For the purposes of this Convention, the term "rural workers" means any person engaged in agriculture, handicrafts or a related occupation in a rural area, whether as a wage earner or, subject to the provisions of paragraph 2 of this Article, as a self-employed person such as a tenant, sharecropper or small owner-occupier.

2.   This Convention applies only to those tenants, share-croppers or small owner-occupiers who derive their main income from agriculture, who work the land themselves with the help only of their family or with the help of occasional outside labour and who do not -

(a)   permanently employ workers; or

(b)   employ a substantial number of seasonal workers; or

(c)   have any land cultivated by sharecroppers or tenants.

Article 3

1.   All categories of rural workers, whether they are wage earners or self-employed, shall have the right to establish and, subject only to the rules of the organisation concerned, to join organisations of their own choosing without previous authorisation.

2.   The principles of freedom of association shall be fully respected; rural workers' organisations shall be independent and voluntary in character and shall remain free from all interference, coercion or repression.

3.   The acquisition of legal personality by organisations of rural workers shall not be made subject to conditions of such a character as to restrict the application of the provisions of the preceding paragraphs of this Article.

4.   In exercising the rights provided for in this Article rural workers and their respective organisations, like other persons or organised collectivities, shall respect the law of the land.

5.   The law of the land shall not be such as to impair, nor shall it be so applied as to impair, the guarantees provided for in this Article.

Article 4

It shall be an objective of national policy concerning rural development to facilitate the establishment and growth, on a voluntary basis, of strong and independent organisations of rural workers as an effective means of ensuring the participation of rural workers, without discrimination as defined in the Discrimination (Employment and Occupation) Convention, 1958, in economic and social development and in the benefits resulting therefrom.

Article 5

1.   In order to enable organisations of rural workers to play their role in economic and social development, each Member which ratifies this Convention shall adopt and carry out a policy of active encouragement to these organisations, particularly with a view to eliminating obstacles to their establishment, their growth and the pursuit of their lawful activities, as well as such legislative and administrative discrimination against rural workers' organisations and their members as may exist.

2.   Each Member which ratifies this Convention shall ensure that national laws or regulations do not, given the special circumstances of the rural sector, inhibit the establishment and growth of rural workers' organisations.

Article 6

Steps shall be taken to promote the widest possible understanding of the need to further the development of rural workers' organisations and of the contribution they can make to improving employment opportunities and general conditions of work and life in rural areas as well as to increasing the national income and achieving a better distribution thereof.

Rural Workers' Organisations Recommendation, 1975
(No. 149)

I. GENERAL PROVISIONS

1. (1) This Recommendation applies to all types of organisations of rural workers, including organisations not restricted to but representative of rural workers.

(2)   The Co-operatives (Developing Countries) Recommendation, 1966, further remains applicable to the organisations of rural workers falling within its scope.

2. (1) For the purposes of this Recommendation, the term "rural workers" means any person engaged in agriculture, handicrafts or related occupation in a rural area, whether as a wage earner or, subject to the provisions of subparagraph (2) of this Paragraph, as a self-employed person such as a tenant, sharecropper or small owner-occupier.

(2)   This Recommendation applies only to those tenants, sharecroppers or small owner-occupiers who derive their main income from agriculture, who work the land themselves, with the help only of their family or with the help of occasional outside labour and who do not -

(a)   permanently employ workers; or

(b)   employ a substantial number of seasonal workers; or

(c)   have any land cultivated by sharecroppers or tenants.

3.   All categories of rural workers, whether they are wage earners or self-employed, should have the right to establish and, subject only to the rules of the organisation concerned, to join organisations of their own choosing without previous authorisation.

II. ROLE OF ORGANISATIONS OF RURAL WORKERS

4.   It should be an objective of national policy concerning
rural development to facilitate the establishment and growth, on a
voluntary basis, of strong and independent organisations of rural
workers as an effective means of ensuring the participation of rural
workers, without discrimination as defined in the Discrimination
(Employment and Occupation) Convention, 1958, in economic and social
development and in the benefits resulting therefrom.

5.   Such organisations should, as appropriate, be able to -

(a)   represent, further and defend the interests of rural workers, for
       instance by undertaking negotiations and consultations at all
       levels on behalf of such workers collectively;

(b)   represent rural workers in connection with the formulation,
       implementation and evaluation of programmes of rural development
       and at all stages and levels of national planning;

(c)   involve the various categories of rural workers, according to the
       interests of each, actively and from the outset in the
       implementation of -

       (i)   programmes of agricultural development, including the
              improvement of techniques of production, storing, pro-
              cessing, transport and marketing;

       (ii)   programmes of agrarian reform, land settlement and land
              development;

       (iii) programmes concerning public works, rural industries and
              rural crafts;

       (iv)   rural development programmes, including those implemented
              with the collaboration of the United Nations, the
              International Labour Organisation and other specialised
              agencies;

       (v)   the information and education programmes and other
              activities referred to in Paragraph 15 of this
              Recommendation;

(d)   promote and obtain access of rural workers to services such as
       credit, supply, marketing and transport as well as to tech-
       nological services;

(e)   play an active part in the improvement of general and vocational
       education and training in rural areas as well as in training for
       community development, training for co-operative and other
       activities of rural workers' organisations and training for the
       management thereof;

(f)   contribute to the improvement of the conditions of work and life
       of rural workers, including occupational safety and health;

(g)   promote the extension of social security and basic social
       services in such fields as housing, health and recreation.

III.   MEANS OF ENCOURAGING THE GROWTH OF
ORGANISATIONS OF RURAL WORKERS

6.   In order to enable organisations of rural workers to play
their role in economic and social development, member States should
adopt and carry out a policy of active encouragement to these
organisations, particularly with a view to -

(a)   eliminating obstacles to their establishment, their growth and
        the pursuit of their lawful activities, as well as such
        legislative and administrative discrimination against rural
        workers' organisations and their members as may exist;

(b)   extending to rural workers' organisations and their members such
        facilities for vocational education and training as are available
        to other workers' organisations and their members; and

(c)   enabling rural workers' organisations to pursue a policy to
        ensure that social and economic protection and benefits
        corresponding to those made available to industrial workers or,
        as appropriate, workers engaged in other non-industrial occupa-
        tions are also extended to their members.

7. (1) The principles of freedom of association should be fully
respected; rural workers' organisations should be independent and
voluntary in character and should remain free from all interference,
coercion or repression.

(2)   The acquisition of legal personality by organisations of
rural workers should not be made subject to conditions of such a
character as to restrict the application of the provisions of Paragraph
3 and subparagraph (1) of this Paragraph.

(3)   In exercising the rights which they enjoy in pursuance of
Paragraph 3 and of this Paragraph rural workers and their respective
organisations, like other persons or organised collectivities, should
respect the law of the land.

(4)   The law of the land should not be such as to impair, nor
should it be so applied as to impair, the guarantees provided for in
Paragraph 3 and in this Paragraph.

A.   Legislative and administrative measures

8. (1) Member States should ensure that national laws or
regulations do not, given the special circumstances of the rural
sector, inhibit the establishment and growth of rural workers'
organisations.

(2)   In particular -

(a)   the principles of right of association and of collective
        bargaining, in conformity especially with the Right of
        Association (Agriculture) Convention, 1921, the Freedom of
        Association and Protection of the Right to Organise Convention,
        1948, and the Right to Organise and Collective Bargaining
        Convention, 1949, should be made fully effective by the

application to the rural sector of general laws or regulations on the subject, or by the adoption of special laws or regulations, full account being taken of the needs of all categories of rural workers;

(b) relevant laws and regulations should be fully adapted to the special needs of rural areas; for instance -

    (i) requirements regarding minimum membership, minimum levels of education and minimum funds should not be permitted to impede the development of organisations in rural areas where the population is scattered, ill educated and poor;

    (ii) problems which may arise concerning the access of organisations of rural workers to their members should be dealt with in a manner respecting the rights of all concerned and in accordance with the terms of the Freedom of Association and Protection of the Right to Organise Convention, 1948, and the Workers' Representatives Convention, 1971;

    (iii) there should be effective protection of the rural workers concerned against dismissal and against eviction which are based on their status or activities as leaders or members of rural workers' organisations.

9. There should be adequate machinery, whether in the form of labour inspection or of special services, or in some other form, to ensure the effective implementation of laws and regulations concerning rural workers' organisations and their membership.

10. (1) Where rural workers find it difficult, under existing conditions, to take the initiative in establishing and operating their own organisations, existing organisations should be encouraged to give them, at their request, appropriate guidance and assistance corresponding to their interests.

(2) Where necessary, such assistance could on request be supplemented by advisory services staffed by persons qualified to give legal and technical advice and to run educational courses.

11. Appropriate measures should be taken to ensure that there is effective consultation and dialogue with rural workers' organisations on all matters relating to conditions of work and life in rural areas.

12. (1) In connection with the formulation and, as appropriate, the application of economic and social plans and programmes and any other general measures concerning the economic, social or cultural development of rural areas, rural workers' organisations should be associated with planning procedures and institutions, such as statutory boards and committees, development agencies and economic and social councils.

(2) In particular, appropriate measures should be taken to make possible the effective participation of such organisations in the formulation, implementation and evaluation of agrarian reform programmes.

13. Member States should encourage the establishment of procedures and institutions which foster contacts between rural workers' organisations, employers and their organisations and the competent authorities.

B. Public information

14.   Steps should be taken, particularly by the competent
authority, to promote -

(a)   the understanding of those directly concerned, such as central,
       local and other authorities, rural employers and landlords, of
       the contribution which can be made by rural workers' organisa-
       tions to the increase and better distribution of national income,
       to the increase of productive and remunerative employment
       opportunities in the rural sector, to the raising of the general
       level of education and training of the various categories of
       rural workers and to the improvement of the general conditions of
       work and life in rural areas;

(b)   the understanding of the general public, including, in
       particular, that in the non-rural sectors of the economy, cf the
       importance of maintaining a proper balance between the
       development of rural and urban areas, and of the desirability, as
       a contribution towards ensuring that balance, of furthering the
       development of rural workers' organisations.

15.   These steps might include -

(a)   mass information and education campaigns, especially with a view
       to giving rural workers full and practical information on their
       rights, so that they may exercise them as necessary;

(b)   radio, television and cinema programmes, and periodic articles in
       the local and national press, describing the conditions of life
       and work in rural areas and explaining the aims of rural workers'
       organisations and the results obtained by their activities;

(c)   the organisation, locally, of seminars and meetings with the
       participation of representatives of the various categories of
       rural workers, of employers and landlords, of cther sectors of
       the population and of local authorities;

(d)   the organisation of visits to rural areas of journalists,
       representatives of employers and workers in industry or commerce,
       students of universities and schools accompanied by their
       teachers, and other representatives of the various sectors of the
       population;

(e)   the preparation of suitable curricula for the various types and
       levels of schools appropriately reflecting the problems of
       agricultural production and the life of rural workers.

C. Education and training

16.   In order to ensure a sound growth of rural workers'
organisations and the rapid assumption of their full role in economic
and social development, steps should be taken, by the competent
authority among others, to -

(a)   impart to the leaders and members of rural workers' organisations
       knowledge of -

(i)   national laws and regulations and international standards
        on questions of direct concern to the activity of the
        organisations, in particular the right of association;

(ii)   the basic principles of the establishment and operation of
        organisations of rural workers;

(iii)   questions regarding rural development as part of the
        economic and social development of the country, including
        agricultural and handicraft production, storing,
        processing, transport, marketing and trade;

(iv)   principles and techniques of national planning at different
        levels;

(v)   training manuals and programmes which are published or
        established by the United Nations, the International Labour
        Organisation or other specialised agencies and which are
        designed for the education and training of rural workers;

(b)   improve and foster the education of rural workers in general,
       technical, economic and social fields, so as to make them better
       able both to develop their organisations and understand their
       rights and to participate actively in rural development;
       particular attention should be paid to the training of wholly or
       partly illiterate workers through literacy programmes linked with
       the practical expansion of their activities;

(c)   promote programmes directed to the role which women can and
       should play in the rural community, integrated in general
       programmes of education and training to which women and men
       should have equal opportunities of access;

(d)   provide training designed particularly for educators of rural
       workers, to enable them, for example, to help in the development
       of co-operative and other appropriate forms of servicing acti-
       vities which would enable organisations to respond directly to
       membership needs while fostering their independence through
       economic self-reliance;

(e)   give support to programmes for the promotion of rural youth in
       general.

        17. (1) As an effective means of providing the training and
education referred to in Paragraph 16, programmes of workers' education
or adult education, specially adapted to national and local conditions
and to the social, economic and cultural needs of the various
categories of rural workers, including the special needs of women and
young persons, should be formulated and applied.

        (2) In view of their special knowledge and experience in these
fields, trade union movements and existing organisations which
represent rural workers might be closely associated with the
formulation and carrying out of such programmes.

                    D. Financial and material assistance

        18. (1) Where, particularly in the initial stages of development,
rural workers' organisations consider that they need financial or

material assistance, for instance to help them in carrying out
programmes of education and training, and where they seek and obtain
such assistance, they should receive it in a manner which fully
respects their independence and interests and those of their members.
Such assistance should be supplementary to the initiative and efforts
of rural workers in financing their own organisations.

(2)   The foregoing principles apply in all cases of financial
and material assistance, including those in which it is the policy of
a member State to render such assistance itself.

APPENDIX II

REPORTS RECEIVED ON 10 MARCH 1983
(Article 19 of the Constitution)

Member States	Convention No. 87	Convention No. 98	Convention No. 141	Recommendation No. 149
Afghanistan	-	-	R	-
Algeria	R	R	X	X
Angola	-	R	-	-
Argentina	R	R	X	X
Australia	R	R	X	X
Austria	R	R	R	X
Bahamas	X	R	X	-
Bahrain	X	X	X	X
Bangladesh	R	R	X	X
Barbados	R	R	X	X
Belgium	R	R	X	X
Benin	R	R	-	-
Bolivia	R	R	-	-
Botswana	-	-	-	-
Brazil	X	R	X	X
Bulgaria	R	R	X	X
Burma	R	-	-	-
Burundi	X	X	X	X
Byelorussian SSR	R	R	X	X
United Republic of Cameroon	R	R	X	X
Canada	R	X	X	X
Cape Verde	X	R	X	X
Central African Republic	R	R	X	-
Chad	R	R	-	-
Chile	X	X	X	X
China	-	R	-	-
Colombia	R	R	X	X
Comoros	R	R	X	-
Congo	R	-	-	-
Costa Rica	R	R	-	-
Cuba	R	R	R	X
Cyprus	R	R	R	X
Czechoslovakia	R	R	X	X
Democratic Yemen	-	R	-	-
Denmark	R	R	R	-
Djibouti	R	R	X	X
Dominican Republic	R	R	X	-
Ecuador	R	R	R	X

Member States	Convention No. 87	Convention No. 98	Convention No. 141	Recommendation No. 149
Egypt	R	R	X	X
El Salvador	X	X	X	X
Equatorial Guinea	-	-	-	-
Ethiopia	R	R	X	X
Fiji	-	R	-	-
Finland	R	R	R	X
France	R	R	X	X
Gabon	R	R	X	X
German Democratic Republic	R	R	X	X
Federal Republic of Germany	R	R	R	X
Ghana	R	R	X	X
Greece	R	R	X	X
Grenada	-	R	-	-
Guatemala	R	R	X	X
Guinea	R	R	-	-
Guinea-Bissau	X	R	X	X
Guyana	R	R	RX	X
Haiti	R	R	X	X
Honduras	R	R	-	-
Hungary	R	R	X	X
Iceland	R	R	X	-
India	X	X	R	X
Indonesia	X	R	X	X
Iran	-	-	-	-
Iraq	-	R	-	-
Ireland	R	R	X	X
Israel	R	R	R	-
Italy	R	R	R	X
Ivory Coast	R	R	-	-
Jamaica	R	R	X	X
Japan	R	R	X	X
Jordan	-	R	-	-
Democratic Kampuchea	-	-	-	-
Kenya	-	R	R	-
Kuwait	R	X	X	X
Lao Republic	-	-	-	-
Lebanon	X	R	X	X
Lesotho	R	R	-	-
Liberia	R	R	X	X
Libyan Arab Jamahiriya	-	R	-	-
Luxembourg	R	R	X	X
Madagascar	R	X	X	X
Malawi	X	R	X	X
Malaysia	X	R	X	X
Mali	R	R	X	X
Malta	R	R	X	X
Mauritania	R	-	-	-
Mauritius	-	R	-	-
Mexico	R	X	R	X
Mongolia	R	R	X	X
Morocco	X	R	X	X
Mozambique	-	-	-	-

Member States	Conven-tion No. 87	Conven-tion No. 98	Conven-tion No. 141	Recommenda-tion No. 149
Namibia	-	-	-	-
Nepal	-	-	-	-
Netherlands	R	X	R	X
New Zealand	X	X	X	X
Nicaragua	R	R	RX	X
Niger	R	R	-	-
Nigeria	R	R	-	-
Norway	R	R	R	X
Pakistan	R	R	X	X
Panama	R	R	X	X
Papua New Guinea	X	R	X	X
Paraguay	R	R	-	-
Peru	R	R	-	-
Philippines	R	R	R	X
Poland	R	R	X	X
Portugal	R	R	X	X
Qatar	X	X	X	X
Romania	R	R	X	X
Rwanda	X	X	X	X
Saint Lucia	R	R	-	-
Saudi Arabia	X	X	X	X
Senegal	R	R	X	X
Seychelles	R	-	-	-
Sierra Leone	R	R	-	-
Singapore	X	R	X	X
Somalia	-	-	-	-
Spain	R	R	R	X
Sri Lanka	X	R	-	-
Sudan	-	R	-	-
Suriname	R	X	X	-
Swaziland	R	R	-	-
Sweden	R	R	R	X
Switzerland	R	X	R	X
Syrian Arab Republic	R	R	-	-
Tanzania	X	R	X	X
Thailand	-	-	-	-
Togo	R	X	X	X
Trinidad and Tobago	R	R	-	-
Tunisia	R	R	X	X
Turkey	X	R	X	X
Uganda	-	R	-	-
Ukrainian SSR	R	R	X	X
United Arab Emirates	-	-	-	-
United Kingdom	R	R	R	X
United States	X	X	X	X
Upper Volta	R	R	X	X
Uruguay	R	R	X	X
USSR	R	R	X	X
Venezuela	RX	R	X	-
Viet Nam	-	-	-	-
Yemen	R	R	-	-
Yugoslavia	R	R	X	X
Zaire	-	R	-	-
Zambia	X	X	R	-
Zimbabwe	X	X	X	X

Note: A total of five reports have been received from the following
non-metropolitan territories: United Kingdom (Bermuda,
Gibraltar, Hong Kong, Montserrat, St. Helena).

R = Ratified Conventions
X = Reports received
- = Reports not received

APPENDIX III

LIST OF STATES THAT HAVE OR HAVE NOT RATIFIED CONVENTIONS NOS. 87, 98, 141

Ratified			Not ratified		
Conv. No. 87	Conv. No. 98	Conv. No. 141	Conv. No. 87	Conv. No. 98	Conv. No. 141
Albania	Albania	Afghanistan	Afghanistan	Afghanistan	Algeria
Algeria	Algeria	Austria	Angola	Bahrain	Angola
Angola	Angola	Cuba	Bahamas	Botswana	Antigua and Barbuda
Antigua and Barbuda	Antigua and Barbuda	Cyprus	Bahrain	Burma	Argentina
Argentina	Argentina	Denmark	Botswana	Burundi	Australia
Australia	Australia	Ecuador	Brazil	Canada	Bahamas
Austria	Austria	Finland	Burundi	Chile	Bahrain
Bangladesh	Bahamas	Germany, Fed. Rep.	Cape Verde	Congo	Bangladesh
Barbados	Bangladesh	Guyana	Chile	El Salvador	Barbados
Belgium	Barbados	India	China	Equatorial Guinea	Belgium
Benin	Belgium	Israel	Dem. Yemen	Guinea	Benin
Bolivia	Benin	Italy	El Salvador	India	Bolivia
Bulgaria	Bolivia	Kenya	Equatorial Guinea	Iran	Botswana
Burma	Brazil	Mexico	Guinea	Dem. Kampuchea	Brazil
Byelorussian SSR	Bulgaria	Netherlands	Fiji	Kuwait	Bulgaria
Cameroon, United Rep. of	Byelorussian SSR	Nicaragua	Grenada	Lao Republic	Burma
Canada	Cameroon, United Rep. of	Norway	Guinea-Bissau	Madagascar	Burundi
Central African Rep.	Cape Verde	Philippines	India	Mauritania	Byelorussian SSR
Chad	Central African Rep.	Spain	Indonesia	Mexico	Cameroon, United Rep. of
Colombia	Chad	Sweden	Iran	Mozambique	Canada
Comoros	China	Switzerland	Iraq	Namibia	Cape Verde
Congo	Colombia	United Kingdom	Jordan	Nepal	Central African Rep.
Costa Rica	Comoros	Zambia	Dem. Kampuchea	Netherlands	Chad
Cuba			Kenya	New Zealand	
			Lao Republic	Qatar	
			Lebanon	Rwanda	

Ratified			Not ratified		
Conv. No. 87	Conv. No. 98	Conv. No. 141	Conv. No. 87	Conv. No. 98	Conv. No. 141
Cyprus	Costa Rica		Libyan Arab Jamahiriya	Saudi Arabia	Chile
Czechoslovakia	Cuba		Malawi	Seychelles	China
Denmark	Cyprus		Malaysia	Somalia	Colombia
Djibouti	Czechoslovakia		Mauritius	Suriname	Comoros
Dominica	Dem. Yemen		Morocco	Switzerland	Congo
Dominican Rep.	Denmark		Mozambique	Thailand	Costa Rica
Ecuador	Djibouti		Namibia	Togo	Czechoslovakia
Egypt	Dominica		Nepal	United Arab Emirates	Dem. Yemen
Ethiopia	Dominican Rep.		New Zealand	United States	Djibouti
Finland	Ecuador		Papua New Guinea	Viet Nam	Dominica
France	Egypt		Qatar	Zambia	Dominican Rep.
Gabon	Ethiopia		Rwanda	Zimbabwe	Egypt
German Dem. Rep.	Fiji		Saudi Arabia		El Salvador
Germany, Fed. Rep.	Finland		Singapore		Equatorial Guinea
Ghana	France		Somalia		Ethiopia
Greece	Gabon		Sri Lanka		Fiji
Guatemala	German Dem. Rep.		Sudan		France
Guinea	Germany, Fed. Rep.		Tanzania		Gabon
Guyana	Ghana		Thailand		German Dem. Rep.
Haiti	Greece		Turkey		Ghana
Honduras	Grenada		Uganda		Greece
Hungary	Guatemala		United Arab Emirates		Grenada
Iceland	Guinea		United States		Guatemala
Ireland	Guinea-Bissau		Viet Nam		Guinea
Israel	Guyana		Zaire		Guinea Bissau
Italy	Haiti		Zimbabwe		Haiti
Ivory Coast	Honduras				Honduras
Jamaica	Hungary				Hungary
Japan	Iceland				Iceland
Kuwait	Indonesia				Indonesia
Lesotho	Iraq				Iran
Liberia	Ireland				

Ratified			Not ratified		
Conv. No. 87	Conv. No. 98	Conv. No. 141	Conv. No. 87	Conv. No. 98	Conv. No. 141
Luxembourg	Israel				Iraq
Madagascar	Italy				Ireland
Mali	Ivory Coast				Ivory Coast
Malta	Jamaica				Jamaica
Mauritania	Japan				Japan
Mexico	Jordan				Jordan
Mongolia	Kenya				Dem. Kampuchea
Netherlands	Lebanon				Kuwait
Nicaragua	Lesotho				Lao Republic
Niger	Liberia				Lebanon
Nigeria	Libyan Arab				Lesotho
Norway	Jamahiriya				Liberia
Pakistan	Luxembourg				Libyan Arab
Panama	Malawi				Jamahiriya
Paraguay	Malaysia				Luxembourg
Peru	Mali				Madagascar
Philippines	Malta				Malawi
Poland	Mauritius				Malaysia
Portugal	Mongolia				Mali
Romania	Morocco				Malta
Senegal	Nicaragua				Mauritania
Seychelles	Niger				Mauritius
Sierra Leone	Nigeria				Mongolia
Spain	Norway				Morocco
Saint Lucia	Pakistan				Mozambique
Suriname	Panama				Namibia
Swaziland	Papua New				Nepal
Sweden	Guinea				New Zealand
Switzerland	Paraguay				Niger
Syrian Arab	Peru				Nigeria
Republic	Philippines				Pakistan
Togo	Poland				Panama
Trinidad and	Portugal				

	Ratified			Not ratified	
Conv. No. 87	Conv. No. 98	Conv. No. 141	Conv. No. 87	Conv. No. 98	Conv. No. 141
Tobago	Romania				Papua New Guinea
Tunisia	Saint Lucia				Paraguay
Ukrainian SSR	Senegal				Peru
USSR	Sierra Leone				Poland
United Kingdom	Singapore				Portugal
Upper Volta	Spain				Qatar
Uruguay	Sri Lanka				Romania
Venezuela	Sudan				Rwanda
Yemen	Swaziland				Saint Lucia
Yugoslavia	Sweden				Saudi Arabia
	Syrian Arab Republic				Senegal
	Tanzania				Seychelles
	Trinidad and Tobago				Sierra Leone
	Tunisia				Singapore
	Turkey				Somalia
	Uganda				Sri Lanka
	Ukrainian SSR				Sudan
	USSR				Suriname
	United Kingdom				Swaziland
	Upper Volta				Syrian Arab Republic
	Uruguay				Tanzania
	Venezuela				Thailand
	Yemen				Togo
	Yugoslavia				Trinidad and Tobago
	Zaire				Tunisia
					Turkey
					Uganda
					Ukrainian SSR
					USSR
					United Arab

	Ratified			Not ratified	
Conv. No. 87	Conv. No. 98	Conv. No. 141	Conv. No. 87	Conv. No. 98	Conv. No. 141
					Emirates
					United States
					Upper Volta
					Uruguay
					Venezuela
					Viet Nam
					Yemen
					Yugoslavia
					Zaire
					Zimbabwe